6. Enter your class ID code to join a class.

IF YOU HAVE A CLASS CODE FROM YOUR TEAC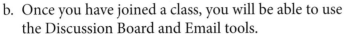

a. Enter your class code and click [**Next**]

b. Once you have joined a class, you will be able to use the Discussion Board and Email tools.

c. To enter this code later, choose **Join a Class**.

IF YOU DO NOT HAVE A CLASS CODE

a. If you do not have a class ID code, click [**Skip**]

b. You do not need a class ID code to use *iQ Online*.

c. To enter this code later, choose **Join a Class**.

7. Review registration information and click Log In. Then choose your book. Click **Activities** to begin using *iQ Online*.

IMPORTANT

- After you register, the next time you want to use *iQ Online*, go to www.iQOnlinePractice.com and log in with your email address and password.
- The online content can be used for 12 months from the date you register.
- For help, please contact customer service: eltsupport@oup.com.

WHAT IS iQ ONLINE ?

All new activities provide essential skills **practice** and support.
Vocabulary and Grammar **games** immerse you in the language and provide even more practice.
Authentic, engaging **videos** generate new ideas and opinions on the Unit Question.

Go to the Media Center to download or stream all **student book audio**.

Use the **Discussion Board** to discuss the Unit Question and more.

Email encourages communication with your teacher and classmates.

Automatic grading gives immediate feedback and tracks progress.
Progress Reports show what you have mastered and where you still need more practice.

SHAPING learning TOGETHER

We would like to acknowledge the teachers from all over the world who participated in the development process and review of the Q series.

Special thanks to our *Q: Skills for Success* Second Edition Topic Advisory Board

Shaker Ali Al-Mohammad, Buraimi University College, Oman; **Dr. Asmaa A. Ebrahim**, University of Sharjah, U.A.E.; **Rachel Batchilder**, College of the North Atlantic, Qatar; **Anil Bayir**, Izmir University, Turkey; **Flora Mcvay Bozkurt**, Maltepe University, Turkey; **Paul Bradley**, University of the Thai Chamber of Commerce Bangkok, Thailand; **Joan Birrell-Bertrand**, University of Manitoba, MB, Canada; **Karen E. Caldwell**, Zayed University, U.A.E.; **Nicole Hammond Carrasquel**, University of Central Florida, FL, U.S.; **Kevin Countryman**, Seneca College of Applied Arts & Technology, ON, Canada; **Julie Crocker**, Arcadia University, NS, Canada; **Marc L. Cummings**, Jefferson Community and Technical College, KY, U.S.; **Rachel DeSanto**, Hillsborough Community College Dale Mabry Campus, FL, U.S.; **Nilüfer Ertürkmen**, Ege University, Turkey; **Sue Fine**, Ras Al Khaimah Women's College (HCT), U.A.E.; **Amina Al Hashami**, Nizwa College of Applied Sciences, Oman; **Stephan Johnson**, Nagoya Shoka Daigaku, Japan; **Sean Kim**, Avalon, South Korea; **Gregory King**, Chubu Daigaku, Japan; **Seran Küçük**, Maltepe University, Turkey; **Jonee De Leon**, VUS, Vietnam; **Carol Lowther**, Palomar College, CA, U.S.; **Erin Harris-MacLead**, St. Mary's University, NS, Canada; **Angela Nagy**, Maltepe University, Turkey; **Huynh Thi Ai Nguyen**, Vietnam; **Daniel L. Paller**, Kinjo Gakuin University, Japan; **Jangyo Parsons**, Kookmin University, South Korea; **Laila Al Qadhi**, Kuwait University, Kuwait; **Josh Rosenberger**, English Language Institute University of Montana, MT, U.S.; **Nancy Schoenfeld**, Kuwait University, Kuwait; **Jenay Seymour**, Hongik University, South Korea; **Moon-young Son**, South Korea; **Matthew Taylor**, Kinjo Gakuin Daigaku, Japan; **Burcu Tezcan-Unal**, Zayed University, U.A.E.; **Troy Tucker**, Edison State College-Lee Campus, FL, U.S.; **Kris Vicca**, Feng Chia University, Taichung; **Jisook Woo**, Incheon University, South Korea; **Dunya Yenidunya**, Ege University, Turkey

UNITED STATES **Marcarena Aguilar**, North Harris College, TX; **Rebecca Andrade**, California State University North Ridge, CA; **Lesley Andrews**, Boston University, MA; **Deborah Anholt**, Lewis and Clark College, OR; **Robert Anzelde**, Oakton Community College, IL; **Arlys Arnold**, University of Minnesota, MN; **Marcia Arthur**, Renton Technical College, WA; **Renee Ashmeade**, Passaic County Community College, NJ; **Anne Bachmann**, Clackamas Community College, OR; **Lida Baker**, UCLA, CA; **Ron Balsamo**, Santa Rosa Junior College, CA; **Lori Barkley**, Portland State University, OR; **Eileen Barlow**, SUNY Albany, NY; **Sue Bartch**, Cuyahoga Community College, OH; **Lora Bates**, Oakton High School, VA; **Barbara Batra**, Nassau County Community College, NY; **Nancy Baum**, University of Texas at Arlington, TX; **Rebecca Beck**, Irvine Valley College, CA; **Linda Berendsen**, Oakton Community College, IL; **Jennifer Binckes Lee**, Howard Community College, MD; **Grace Bishop**, Houston Community College, TX; **Jean W. Bodman**, Union County College, NJ; **Virginia Bouchard**, George Mason University, VA; **Kimberley Briesch Sumner**, University of Southern California, CA; **Kevin Brown**, University of California, Irvine, CA; **Laura Brown**, Glendale Community College, CA; **Britta Burton**, Mission College, CA; **Allison L. Callahan**, Harold Washington College, IL; **Gabriela Cambiasso**, Harold Washington College, IL; **Jackie Campbell**, Capistrano Unified School District, CA; **Adele C. Camus**, George Mason University, VA; **Laura Chason**, Savannah College, GA; **Kerry Linder Catana**, Language Studies International, NY; **An Cheng**, Oklahoma State University, OK; **Carole Collins**, North Hampton Community College, PA; **Betty R. Compton**, Intercultural Communications College, HI; **Pamela Couch**, Boston University, MA; **Fernanda Crowe**, Intrax International Institute, CA; **Vicki Curtis**, Santa Cruz, CA; **Margo Czinski**, Washtenaw Community College, MI; **David Dahnke**, Lone Star College, TX; **Gillian M. Dale**, CA; **L. Dalgish**, Concordia College, MN; **Christopher Davis**, John Jay College, NY; **Sherry Davis**, Irvine University, CA; **Natalia de Cuba**, Nassau County Community College, NY; **Sonia Delgadillo**, Sierra College, CA; **Esmeralda Diriye**, Cypress College & Cal Poly, CA; **Marta O. Dmytrenko-Ahrabian**, Wayne State University, MI; **Javier Dominguez**, Central High School, SC; **Jo Ellen Downey-Greer**, Lansing Community College, MI; **Jennifer Duclos**, Boston University, MA; **Yvonne Duncan**, City College of San Francisco, CA; **Paul Dydman**, USC Language Academy, CA; **Anna Eddy**, University of Michigan-Flint, MI; **Zohan El-Gamal**, Glendale Community College, CA; **Jennie Farnell**, University of Connecticut, CT; **Susan Fedors**, Howard Community College, MD; **Valerie Fiechter**, Mission College, CA; **Ashley Fifer**, Nassau County Community College, NY; **Matthew Florence**, Intrax International Institute, CA; **Kathleen Flynn**, Glendale College, CA; **Elizabeth Fonsea**, Nassau County Community College, NY; **Eve Fonseca**, St. Louis Community College, MO; **Elizabeth Foss**, Washtenaw Community College, MI; **Duff C. Galda**, Pima Community College, AZ; **Christiane Galvani**, Houston Community College, TX; **Gretchen Gerber**, Howard Community College, MD; **Ray Gonzalez**, Montgomery College, MD; **Janet Goodwin**, University of California, Los Angeles, CA; **Alyona Gorokhova**, Grossmont College, CA; **John Graney**, Santa Fe College, FL; **Kathleen Green**, Central High School, AZ; **Nancy Hamadou**, Pima Community College-West Campus, AZ; **Webb Hamilton**, De Anza College, San Jose City College, CA; **Janet Harclerode**, Santa Monica Community College, CA; **Sandra Hartmann**, Language and Culture Center, TX; **Kathy Haven**, Mission College, CA; **Roberta Hendrick**, Cuyahoga Community College, OH; **Ginny Heringer**, Pasadena City College, CA; **Adam Henricksen**, University of Maryland, MD; **Carolyn Ho**, Lone Star College-CyFair, TX; **Peter Hoffman**, LaGuardia Community College, NY; **Linda Holden**, College of Lake County, IL; **Jana Holt**, Lake Washington Technical College, WA; **Antonio Iccarino**, Boston University, MA; **Gail Ibele**, University of Wisconsin, WI; **Nina Ito**, American Language Institute, CSU Long Beach, CA; **Linda Jensen**, UCLA, CA; **Lisa Jurkowitz**, Pima Community College, CA; **Mandy Kama**, Georgetown University, Washington, DC; **Stephanie Kasuboski**, Cuyahoga Community College, OH; **Chigusa Katoku**, Mission College, CA; **Sandra Kawamura**, Sacramento City College, CA; **Gail Kellersberger**, University of Houston-Downtown, TX; **Jane Kelly**, Durham Technical Community College, NC; **Maryanne Kildare**, Nassau County Community College, NY; **Julie Park Kim**, George Mason University, VA; **Kindra Kinyon**, Los Angeles Trade-Technical College, CA; **Matt Kline**, El Camino College, CA; **Lisa Kovacs-Morgan**, University of California, San Diego, CA; **Claudia Kupiec**, DePaul University, IL; **Renee La Rue**, Lone Star College-Montgomery, TX; **Janet Langon**, Glendale College, CA; **Lawrence Lawson**, Palomar College, CA; **Rachele Lawton**, The Community College of Baltimore County, MD; **Alice Lee**, Richland College, TX; **Esther S. Lee**, CSUF & Mt. SAC, CA; **Cherie Lenz-Hackett**, University of Washington, WA; **Joy Leventhal**, Cuyahoga Community College, OH; **Alice Lin**, UCI Extension, CA; **Monica Lopez**, Cerritos College, CA; **Dustin Lovell**, FLS International Marymount College, CA; **Carol Lowther**, Palomar College, CA; **Candace Lynch-Thompson**, North Orange County Community College District, CA; **Thi Thi Ma**, City College of San Francisco, CA; **Steve Mac Isaac**, USC Long Academy, CA; **Denise Maduli-Williams**, City College of San Francisco, CA; **Eileen Mahoney**, Camelback High School, AZ; **Naomi Mardock**, MCC-Omaha, NE; **Brigitte Maronde**, Harold Washington College, IL; **Marilyn Marquis**, Laposita College CA; **Doris Martin**, Glendale Community College; Pasadena City College, CA; **Keith Maurice**, University of Texas at Arlington, TX; **Nancy Mayer**, University of Missouri-St. Louis, MO; **Aziah McNamara**, Kansas State University, KS; **Billie McQuillan**, Education Heights, MN; **Karen Merritt**, Glendale Union High School District, AZ; **Holly Milkowart**, Johnson County Community College, KS; **Eric Moyer**, Intrax International Institute, CA; **Gino Muzzatti**, Santa Rosa Junior College, CA; **Sandra Navarro**, Glendale Community College, CA; **Than Nyeinkhin**, ELAC, PCC, CA; **William Nedrow**, Triton College, IL; **Eric Nelson**, University of Minnesota, MN; **Than Nyeinkhin**, ELAC, PCC, CA; **Fernanda Ortiz**, Center for English as a Second Language at the University of Arizona, AZ; **Rhony Ory**, Ygnacio Valley High School, CA; **Paul Parent**, Montgomery College, MD; **Dr. Sumeeta Patnaik**, Marshall University, W.V.; **Oscar Pedroso**, Miami Dade College, FL; **Robin Persiani**, Sierra College, CA; **Patricia Prenz-Belkin**, Hostos Community College, NY; **Suzanne Powell**, University of Louisville, KY; **Jim Ranalli**, Iowa State University, IA; **Toni R. Randall**, Santa Monica College, CA; **Vidya Rangachari**, Mission College, CA; **Elizabeth Rasmussen**, Northern Virginia Community College, VA; **Lara Ravitch**, Truman College, IL;

Deborah Repasz, San Jacinto College, TX; Marisa Recinos, English Language Center, Brigham Young University, UT; Andrey Reznikov, Black Hills State University, SD; Alison Rice, Hunter College, NY; Jennifer Robles, Ventura Unified School District, CA; Priscilla Rocha, Clark County School District, NV; Dzidra Rodins, DePaul University, IL; Maria Rodriguez, Central High School, AZ; Josh Rosenberger, English Language Institute University of Montana, MT; Alice Rosso, Bucks County Community College, PA; Rita Rozzi, Xavier University, OH; Maria Ruiz, Victor Valley College, CA; Kimberly Russell, Clark College, WA; Stacy Sabraw, Michigan State University, MI; Irene Sakk, Northwestern University, IL; Deborah Sandstrom, University of Illinois at Chicago, IL; Jenni Santamaria, ABC Adult, CA; Shaeley Santiago, Ames High School, IA; Peg Sarosy, San Francisco State University, CA; Alice Savage, North Harris College, TX; Donna Schaeffer, University of Washington, WA; Karen Marsh Schaeffer, University of Utah, UT; Carol Schinger, Northern Virginia Community College, VA; Robert Scott, Kansas State University, KS; Suell Scott, Sheridan Technical Center, FL; Shira Seaman, Global English Academy, NY; Richard Seltzer, Glendale Community College, CA; Harlan Sexton, CUNY Queensborough Community College, NY; Kathy Sherak, San Francisco State University, CA; German Silva, Miami Dade College, FL; Ray Smith, Maryland English Institute, University of Maryland, MD; Shira Smith, NICE Program University of Hawaii, HI; Tara Smith, Felician College, NJ; Monica Snow, California State University, Fullerton, CA; Elaine Soffer, Nassau County Community College, NY; Andrea Spector, Santa Monica Community College, CA; Jacqueline Sport, LBWCC Luverne Center, AL; Karen Stanely, Central Piedmont Community College, NC; Susan Stern, Irvine Valley College, CA; Ayse Stromsdorfer, Soldan I.S.H.S., MO; Yilin Sun, South Seattle Community College, WA; Thomas Swietlik, Intrax International Institute, IL; Nicholas Taggert, University of Dayton, OH; Judith Tanka, UCLA Extension–American Language Center, CA; Amy Taylor, The University of Alabama Tuscaloosa, AL; Andrea Taylor, San Francisco State, CA; Priscilla Taylor, University of Southern California, CA; Ilene Teixeira, Fairfax County Public Schools, VA; Shirl H. Terrell, Collin College, TX; Marya Teutsch-Dwyer, St. Cloud State University, MN; Stephen Thergesen, ELS Language Centers, CO; Christine Tierney, Houston Community College, TX; Arlene Turini, North Moore High School, NC; Cara Tuzzolino, Nassau County Community College, NY; Suzanne Van Der Valk, Iowa State University, IA; Nathan D. Vasarhely, Ygnacio Valley High School, CA; Naomi S. Verratti, Howard Community College, MD; Hollyahna Vettori, Santa Rosa Junior College, CA; Julie Vorholt, Lewis & Clark College, OR; Danielle Wagner, FLS International Marymount College, CA; Lynn Walker, Coastline College, CA; Laura Walsh, City College of San Francisco, CA; Andrew J. Watson, The English Bakery; Donald Weasenforth, Collin College, TX; Juliane Widner, Sheepshead Bay High School, NY; Lynne Wilkins, Mills College, CA; Pamela Williams, Ventura College, CA; Jeff Wilson, Irvine Valley College, CA; James Wilson, Consomnes River College, CA; Katie Windahl, Cuyahoga Community College, OH; Dolores "Lorrie" Winter, California State University at Fullerton, CA; Jody Yamamoto, Kapi'olani Community College, HI; Ellen L. Yaniv, Boston University, MA; Norman Yoshida, Lewis & Clark College, OR; Joanna Zadra, American River College, CA; Florence Zysman, Santiago Canyon College, CA;

CANADA Patricia Birch, Brandon University, MB; Jolanta Caputa, College of New Caledonia, BC; Katherine Coburn, UBC's ELI, BC; Erin Harris-Macleod, St. Mary's University, NS; Tami Moffatt, English Language Institute, BC; Kim Papple, Brock University, ON; Robin Peace, Confederation College, BC;

ASIA Rabiatu Abubakar, Eton Language Centre, Malaysia; Wiwik Andreani, Bina Nusantara University, Indonesia; Frank Bailey, Baiko Gakuin University, Japan; Mike Baker, Kosei Junior High School, Japan; Leonard Barrow, Kanto Junior College, Japan; Herman Bartelen, Japan; Siren Betty, Fooyin University, Kaohsiung; Thomas E. Bieri, Nagoya College, Japan; Natalie Brezden, Global English House, Japan; MK Brooks, Mukogawa Women's University, Japan; Truong Ngoc Buu, The Youth Language School, Vietnam; Charles Cabell, Toyo University, Japan; Fred Carruth, Matsumoto University, Japan; Frances Causer, Seijo University, Japan; Jeffrey Chalk, SNU, South Korea; Deborah Chang, Wenzao Ursuline College of Languages, Kaohsiung; David Chatham, Ritsumeikan University, Japan; Andrew Chih Hong Chen, National Sun Yat-sen University, Kaohsiung; Christina Chen, Yu-Tsai Bilingual Elementary School, Taipei; Hui-chen Chen, Shi-Lin High School of Commerce, Taipei; Seungmoon Choe, K2M Language Institute, South Korea; Jason Jeffree Cole, Coto College, Japan; Le Minh Cong, Vungtau Tourism Vocational College, Vietnam; Todd Cooper, Toyama National College of Technology, Japan; Marie Cosgrove, Daito Bunka University, Japan; Randall Cotten, Gifu City Women's College, Japan; Tony Cripps, Ritsumeikan University, Japan; Andy Cubalit, CHS, Thailand; Daniel Cussen, Takushoku University, Japan; Le Dan, Ho Chi Minh City Electric Power College, Vietnam; Simon Daykin, Banghwa-dong Community Centre, South Korea; Aimee Denham, ILA, Vietnam; Bryan Dickson, David's English Center, Taipei; Nathan Ducker, Japan University, Japan; Ian Duncan, Simul International Corporate Training, Japan; Nguyen Thi Kieu Dung, Thang Long University, Vietnam; Truong Quang Dung, Tien Giang University, Vietnam; Nguyen Thi Thuy Duong, Vietnamese American Vocational Training College, Vietnam; Wong Tuck Ee, Raja Tun Azlan Science Secondary School, Malaysia; Emilia Effendy, International Islamic University Malaysia, Malaysia; Bettizza Escueta, KMUTT, Thailand; Robert Eva, Kaisei Girls High School, Japan; Jim George, Luna International Language School, Japan; Jurgen Germeys, Silk Road Language Center, South Korea; Wong Ai Gnoh, SMJK Chung Hwa Confucian, Malaysia; Sarah Go, Seoul Women's University, South Korea; Peter Goosselink, Hokkai High School, Japan; Robert Gorden, SNU, South Korea; Wendy M. Gough, St. Mary College/Nunoike Gaigo Senmon Gakko, Japan; Tim Grose, Sapporo Gakuin University, Japan; Pham Thu Ha, Le Van Tam Primary School, Vietnam; Ann-Marie Hadzima, Taipei; Troy Hammond, Tokyo Gakugei University International Secondary School, Japan; Robiatul 'Adawiah Binti Hamzah, SMK Putrajaya Precinct 8(1), Malaysia; Tran Thi Thuy Hang, Ho Chi Minh City Banking University, Vietnam; To Thi Hong Hanh, CEFALT, Vietnam; George Hays, Tokyo Kokusai Daigaku, Japan; Janis Hearn, Hongik University, South Korea; Chantel Hemmi, Jochi Daigaku, Japan; David Hindman, Sejong University, South Korea; Nahn Cam Hoa, Ho Chi Minh City University of Technology, Vietnam; Jana Holt, Korea University, South Korea; Jason Hollowell, Nihon University, Japan; F. N. (Zoe) Hsu, National Tainan University, Yong Kang; Kuei-ping Hsu, National Tsing Hua University, Hsinchu City; Wenhua Hsu, I-Shou University, Kaohsiung; Luu Nguyen Quoc Hung, Cantho University, Vietnam; Cecile Hwang, Changwon National University, South Korea; Ainol Haryati Ibrahim, Universiti Malaysia Pahang, Malaysia; Robert Jeens, Yonsei University, South Korea; Linda M. Joyce, Kyushu Sangyo University, Japan; Dr. Nisai Kaewsanchai, English Square Kanchanaburi, Thailand; Aniza Kamarulzaman, Sabah Science Secondary School, Malaysia; Ikuko Kashiwabara, Osaka Electro-Communication University, Japan; Gurmit Kaur, INTI College, Malaysia; Nick Keane, Japan; Ward Ketcheson, Aomori University, Japan; Nicholas Kemp, Kyushu International University, Japan; Montchatry Ketmuni, Rajamangala University of Technology, Thailand; Dinh Viet Khanh, Vietnam; Seonok Kim, Kangsu Jongro Language School, South Korea; Suyeon Kim, Anyang University, South Korea; Kelly P. Kimura, Soka University, Japan; Masakazu Kimura, Katoh Gakuen Gyoshu High School, Japan; Gregory King, Chubu Daigaku, Japan; Stan Kirk, Konan University, Japan; Donald Knight, Nan Hua/Fu Li Junior High Schools, Hsinchu; Kari J. Kostiainen, Nagoya City University, Japan; Pattri Kuanpulpol, Silpakorn University, Thailand; Ha Thi Lan, Thai Binh Teacher Training College, Vietnam; Eric Edwin Larson, Miyazaki Prefectural Nursing University, Japan; David Laurence, Chubu Daigaku, Japan; Richard S. Lavin, Prefectural University of Kumamoto, Japan; Shirley Leane, Chugoku Junior College, Japan; I-Hsiu Lee, Yunlin; Nari Lee, Park Jung PLS, South Korea; Tae Lee, Yonsei University, South Korea; Lys Yongsoon Lee, Reading Town Geumcheon, South Korea; Mallory Leece, Sun Moon University, South Korea; Dang Hong Lien, Tan Lam Upper Secondary School, Vietnam; Huang Li-Han, Rebecca Education Institute, Taipei; Sovannarith Lim, Royal University of Phnom Penh, Cambodia; Ginger Lin, National Kaohsiung Hospitality College, Kaohsiung; Noel Lineker, New Zealand/Japan; Tran Dang Khanh Linh, Nha Trang Teachers' Training College, Vietnam; Daphne Liu, Buliton English School, Taipei; S. F. Josephine Liu, Tien-Mu Elementary School, Taipei ; Caroline Luo, Tunghai University, Taichung; Jeng-Jia Luo, Tunghai University, Taichung; Laura MacGregor, Gakushuin University, Japan; Amir Madani, Visuttharangsi School, Thailand; Elena Maeda, Sacred Heart Professional Training College, Japan; Vu Thi Thanh Mai, Hoang Gia Education Center, Vietnam; Kimura Masakazu, Kato Gakuen Gyoshu High School, Japan; Susumu Matsuhashi, Net Link English School, Japan; James McCrostie, Daito Bunka University, Japan; Joel McKee, Inha University, South Korea; Colin McKenzie, Wachirawit Primary School, Thailand; Terumi Miyazoe, Tokyo Denki Daigaku, Japan; William K. Moore, Hiroshima Kokusai Gakuin University, Japan; Kevin Mueller, Tokyo Kokusai Daigaku, Japan; Hudson Murrell, Baiko Gakuin University, Japan; Frances Namba, Senri International School of Kwansei Gakuin, Japan; Keiichi Narita, Niigata University, Japan; Kim Chung Nguyen, Ho Chi Minh University of

Industry, Vietnam; **Do Thi Thanh Nhan**, Hanoi University, Vietnam; **Dale Kazuo Nishi**, Aoyama English Conversation School, Japan; **Huynh Thi Ai Nguyen**, Vietnam; **Dongshin Oh**, YBM PLS, South Korea; **Keiko Okada**, Dokkyo Daigaku, Japan; **Louise Ohashi**, Shukutoku University, Japan; **Yongjun Park**, Sangji University, South Korea; **Donald Patnaude**, Ajarn Donald's English Language Services, Thailand; **Virginia Peng**, Ritsumeikan University, Japan; **Suangkanok Piboonthamnont**, Rajamangala University of Technology, Thailand; **Simon Pitcher**, Business English Teaching Services, Japan; **John C. Probert**, New Education Worldwide, Thailand; **Do Thi Hoa Quyen**, Ton Duc Thang University, Vietnam; **John P. Racine**, Dokkyo University, Japan; **Kevin Ramsden**, Kyoto University of Foreign Studies, Japan; **Luis Rappaport**, Cung Thieu Nha Ha Noi, Vietnam; **Lisa Reshad**, Konan Daigaku Hyogo, Japan; **Peter Riley**, Taisho University, Japan; **Thomas N. Robb**, Kyoto Sangyo University, Japan; **Rory Rosszell**, Meiji Daigaku, Japan; **Maria Feti Rosyani**, Universitas Kristen Indonesia, Indonesia; **Greg Rouault**, Konan University, Japan; **Chris Ruddenklau**, Kindai University, Japan; **Hans-Gustav Schwartz**, Thailand; **Mary-Jane Scott**, Soongsil University, South Korea; **Dara Sheahan**, Seoul National University, South Korea; **James Sherlock**, A.P.W. Angthong, Thailand; **Prof. Shieh**, Minghsin University of Science & Technology, Xinfeng; **Yuko Shimizu**, Ritsumeikan University, Japan; **Suzila Mohd Shukor**, Universiti Sains Malaysia, Malaysia; **Stephen E. Smith**, Mahidol University, Thailand; **Moon-young Son**, South Korea; **Seunghee Son**, Anyang University, South Korea; **Mi-young Song**, Kyungwon University, South Korea; **Lisa Sood**, VUS, BIS, Vietnam; **Jason Stewart**, Taejon International Language School, South Korea; **Brian A. Stokes**, Korea University, South Korea; **Mulder Su**, Shih-Chien University, Kaohsiung; **Yoomi Suh**, English Plus, South Korea; **Yun-Fang Sun**, Wenzao Ursuline College of Languages, Kaohsiung; **Richard Swingle**, Kansai Gaidai University, Japan; **Sanford Taborn**, Kinjo Gakuin Daigaku, Japan; **Mamoru Takahashi**, Akita Prefectural University, Japan; **Tran Hoang Tan**, School of International Training, Vietnam; **Takako Tanaka**, Doshisha University, Japan; **Jeffrey Taschner**, American University Alumni Language Center, Thailand; **Matthew Taylor**, Kinjo Gakuin Daigaku, Japan; **Michael Taylor**, International Pioneers School, Thailand; **Kampanart Thammaphati**, Wattana Wittaya Academy, Thailand; **Tran Duong The**, Sao Mai Language Center, Vietnam; **Tran Dinh Tho**, Duc Tri Secondary School, Vietnam; **Huynh Thi Anh Thu**, Nhatrang College of Culture Arts and Tourism, Vietnam; **Peter Timmins**, Peter's English School, Japan; **Fumie Togano**, Hosei Daini High School, Japan; **F. Sigmund Topor**, Keio University Language School, Japan; **Tu Trieu**, Rise VN, Vietnam; **Yen-Cheng Tseng**, Chang-Jung Christian University, Tainan; **Pei-Hsuan Tu**, National Cheng Kung University, Tainan City; **Hajime Uematsu**, Hirosaki University, Japan; **Rachel Um**, Mok-dong Oedae English School, South Korea; **David Underhill**, EEExpress, Japan; **Ben Underwood**, Kugenuma High School, Japan; **Siriluck Usaha**, Sripatum University, Thailand; **Tyas Budi Utami**, Indonesia; **Nguyen Thi Van**, Far East International School, Vietnam; **Stephan Van Eycken**, Kosei Gakuen Girls High School, Japan; **Zisa Velasquez**, Taihu International School/Semarang International School, China/Indonesia; **Jeffery Walter**, Sangji University, South Korea; **Bill White**, Kinki University, Japan; **Yohanes De Deo Widyastoko**, Xaverius Senior High School, Indonesia; **Dylan Williams**, SNU, South Korea; **Jisuk Woo**, Ichean University, South Korea; **Greg Chung-Hsien Wu**, Providence University, Taichung; **Xun Xiaoming**, BLCU, China; **Hui-Lien Yeh**, Chai Nan University of Pharmacy and Science, Tainan; **Sittiporn Yodnil**, Huachiew Chalermprakiet University, Thailand; **Shamshul Helmy Zambahri**, Universiti Teknologi Malaysia, Malaysia; **Ming-Yuli**, Chang Jung Christian University, Tainan; **Aimin Fadhlee bin Mahmud Zuhodi**, Kuala Terengganu Science School, Malaysia;

TURKEY **Shirley F. Akis**, American Culture Association/Fomara; **Gül Akkoç**, Boğaziçi University; **Seval Akmeşe**, Haliç University; **Ayşenur Akyol**, Ege University; **Ayşe Umut Aribaş**, Beykent University; **Gökhan Asan**, Kapadokya Vocational College; **Hakan Asan**, Kapadokya Vocational College; **Julia Asan**, Kapadokya Vocational College; **Azarvan Atac**, Piri Reis University; **Nur Babat**, Kapadokya Vocational College; **Feyza Balakbabalar**, Kadir Has University; **Gözde Balikçi**, Beykent University; **Deniz Balım**, Haliç University; **Asli Başdoğan**, Kadir Has University; **Ayla Bayram**, Kapadokya Vocational College; **Pinar Bilgiç**, Kadir Has University; **Kenan Bozkurt**, Kapadokya Vocational College; **Yonca Bozkurt**, Ege University; **Frank Carr**, Piri Reis; **Mengü Noyan Çengel**, Ege University; **Elif Doğan**, Ege University; **Natalia Donmez**, 29 Mayis Üniversite; **Nalan Emirsoy**, Kadir Has University; **Ayşe Engin**, Kadir Has University; **Ayhan Gedikbaş**, Ege University; **Gülşah Gençer**, Beykent University; **Seyit Ömer Gök**, Gediz University; **Tuğba Gök**, Gediz University; **İlkay Gökçe**, Ege University; **Zeynep Birinci Guler**, Maltepe University; **Neslihan Güler**, Kadir Has University; **Sircan Gümüş**, Kadir Has University; **Nesrin Gündoğu**, T.C. Piri Reis University; **Tanju Gurpinar**, Piri Reis University; **Selin Gurturk**, Piri Reis University; **Neslihan Gurutku**, Piri Reis University; **Roger Hewitt**, Maltepe University; **Nilüfer İbrahimoğlu**, Beykent University; **Nevin Kaftelen**, Kadir Has University; **Sultan Kalin**, Kapadokya Vocational College; **Sema Kaplan Karabina**, Anadolu University; **Eray Kara**, Giresun University; **Beylü Karayazgan**, Ege University; **Darren Kelso**, Piri Reis University; **Trudy Kittle**, Kapadokya Vocational College; **Şaziye Konaç**, Kadir Has University; **Güneş Korkmaz**, Kapadokya Vocational College; **Robert Ledbury**, Izmir University of Economics; **Ashley Lucas**, Maltepe University; **Bülent Nedium Uça**, Dogus University; **Murat Nurlu**, Ege University; **Mollie Owens**, Kadir Has University; **Oya Özağaç**, Boğaziçi University; **Funda Özcan**, Ege University; **İlkay Özdemir**, Ege University; **Ülkü Öztürk**, Gediz University; **Cassondra Puls**, Anadolu University; **Yelda Sarikaya**, Cappadocia Vocational College; **Müge Şekercioğlu**, Ege University; **Melis Senol**, Canakkale Onsekiz Mart University, The School of Foreign Languages; **Patricia Sümer**, Kadir Has University; **Rex Surface**, Beykent University; **Mustafa Torun**, Kapadokya Vocational College; **Tansel Üstünloğlu**, Ege University; **Fatih Yücel**, Beykent University; **Şule Yüksel**, Ege University;

THE MIDDLE EAST **Amina Saif Mohammed Al Hashamia**, Nizwa College of Applied Sciences, Oman; **Jennifer Baran**, Kuwait University, Kuwait; **Phillip Chappells**, GEMS Modern Academy, U.A.E.; **Sharon Ruth Devaneson**, Ibri College of Technology, Oman; **Hanaa El-Deeb**, Canadian International College, Egypt; **Yvonne Eaton**, Community College of Qatar, Qatar; **Brian Gay**, Sultan Qaboos University, Oman; **Gail Al Hafidh**, Sharjah Women's College (HCT), U.A.E.; **Jonathan Hastings**, American Language Center, Jordan; **Laurie Susan Hilu**, English Language Centre, University of Bahrain, Bahrain; **Abraham Irannezhad**, Mehre Aval, Iran; **Kevin Kempe**, CNA-Q, Qatar; **Jill Newby James**, University of Nizwa; **Mary Kay Klein**, American University of Sharjah, U.A.E.; **Sian Khoury**, Fujairah Women's College (HCT), U.A.E.; **Hussein Dehghan Manshadi**, Farhang Pajooh & Jaam-e-Jam Language School, Iran; **Jessica March**, American University of Sharjah, U.A.E.; **Neil McBeath**, Sultan Qaboos University, Oman; **Sandy McDonagh**, Abu Dhabi Men's College (HCT), U.A.E.; **Rob Miles**, Sharjah Women's College (HCT), U.A.E.; **Michael Kevin Neumann**, Al Ain Men's College (HCT), U.A.E.;

LATIN AMERICA **Aldana Aguirre**, Argentina; **Claudia Almeida**, Coordenação de Idiomas, Brazil; **Cláudia Arias**, Brazil; **Maria de los Angeles Barba**, FES Acatlan UNAM, Mexico; **Lilia Barrios**, Universidad Autónoma de Tamaulipas, Mexico; **Adán Beristain**, UAEM, Mexico; **Ricardo Böck**, Manoel Ribas, Brazil; **Edson Braga**, CNA, Brazil; **Marli Buttelli**, Mater et Magistra, Brazil; **Alessandra Campos**, Inova Centro de Linguas, Brazil; **Priscila Catta Preta Ribeiro**, Brazil; **Gustavo Cestari**, Access International School, Brazil; **Walter D'Alessandro**, Virginia Language Center, Argentina; **Lilian De Gennaro**, Argentina; **Mônica De Stefani**, Quality Centro de Idiomas, Brazil; **Julio Alejandro Flores**, BUAP, Mexico; **Mirian Freire**, CNA Vila Guilherme, Brazil; **Francisco Garcia**, Colegio Lestonnac de San Angel, Mexico; **Miriam Giovanardi**, Brazil; **Darlene Gonzalez Miy**, ITESM CCV, Mexico; **Maria Laura Grimaldi**, Argentina; **Luz Dary Guzmán**, IMPAHU, Colombia; **Carmen Koppe**, Brazil; **Monica Krutzler**, Brazil; **Marcus Murilo Lacerda**, Seven Idiomas, Brazil; **Nancy Lake**, CEL-LEP, Brazil; **Cris Lazzerini**, Brazil; **Sandra Luna**, Argentina; **Ricardo Luvisan**, Brazil; **Jorge Murilo Menezes**, ACBEU, Brazil; **Monica Navarro**, Instituto Cultural A. C., Mexico; **Joacyr Oliveira**, Faculdades Metropolitanas Unidas and Summit School for Teachers, Brazil; **Ayrton Cesar Oliveira de Araujo**, E&A English Classes, Brazil; **Ana Laura Oriente**, Seven Idiomas, Brazil; **Adelia Peña Clavel**, CELE UNAM, Mexico; **Beatriz Pereira**, Summit School, Brazil; **Miguel Perez**, Instituto Cultural, Mexico; **Cristiane Perone**, Associação Cultura Inglesa, Brazil; **Pamela Claudia Pogré**, Colegio Integral Caballito / Universidad de Flores, Argentina; **Dalva Prates**, Brazil; **Marianne Rampaso**, Iowa Idiomas, Brazil; **Daniela Rutolo**, Instituto Superior Cultural Británico, Argentina; **Maione Sampaio**, Maione Carrijo Consultoria em Inglês Ltda, Brazil; **Elaine Santesso**, TS Escola de Idiomas, Brazil; **Camila Francisco Santos**, UNS Idiomas, Brazil; **Lucia Silva**, Cooplem Idiomas, Brazil; **Maria Adela Sorzio**, Instituto Superior Santa Cecilia, Argentina; **Elcio Souza**, Unibero, Brazil; **Willie Thomas**, Rainbow Idiomas, Brazil; **Sandra Villegas**, Instituto Humberto de Paolis, Argentina; **John Whelan**, La Universidad Nacional Autonoma de Mexico, Mexico

CONTENTS

READING ▶ skimming
VOCABULARY ▶ using the dictionary
WRITING ▶ unity in a paragraph
GRAMMAR ▶ comparative and superlative adjectives

UNIT QUESTION

What makes a family business successful?

A Discuss these questions with your classmates.

1. Do you know anyone who owns a family business? What kind of business is it? Do you think it is successful?

2. Look at the photo. Who are the people? What can make this type of business successful?

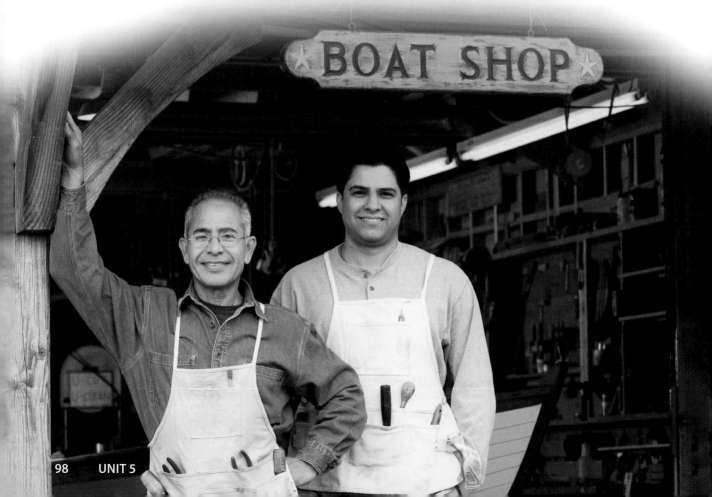

⏵ **B** Listen to *The Q Classroom* online. Then answer these questions.

1. According to Sophy, why is her uncle's business successful?

2. Do you think family members are better employees? Why or why not?

 C Go online to watch the video about a family business that makes zippers. Then check your comprehension.

VIDEO VOCABULARY

founded *(v.)* began

asserted *(v.)* said that something is true

come in *(phr. v.)* finish

open and shut case *(phr. n.)* a strong argument in favor of something

 D Go to the Online Discussion Board to discuss the Unit Question with your classmates.

E Look at the photos. Match the letter of the photo with the correct quotation. Then discuss the meaning of each quotation with your classmates.

____ 1. The family that plays together, stays together. — *Common proverb*

____ 2. True happiness is three generations living under one roof.
— *Chinese proverb*

____ 3. A man should never neglect his family for business. — *Walt Disney*

____ 4. It's more important to know where your children are tonight than where your ancestors were a hundred years ago. — *Anonymous*

F Discuss these questions with a partner.

1. Do you know any families that have three generations (children, parents, grandparents) living in the same house? How do they get along?

2. Do you know any people who put their work before their families? How does this affect the families?

READING 1 | Family Unity Builds Success

You are going to read a magazine article about a successful family business. Use the article to gather information and ideas for your Unit Assignment.

PREVIEW THE READING

Tip for Success

When you read a new word, remember to use the context of the sentence to help you figure out the meaning.

A. VOCABULARY Here are some words from Reading 1. Read their definitions. Then complete each sentence.

> **corporation** (*noun*) a big company
>
> **courage** (*noun*) 🔑 not being afraid or not showing that you are afraid when you do something dangerous or difficult
>
> **design** (*verb*) 🔑 to plan and develop how something will look
>
> **expand** (*verb*) 🔑 to become bigger, or make something become bigger
>
> **expert** (*noun*) 🔑 a person who knows a lot about something
>
> **manage** (*verb*) 🔑 to control someone or something
>
> **strength** (*noun*) 🔑 a good quality or ability that someone or something has
>
> **unity** (*noun*) a situation in which people are working together or in agreement

🔑 Oxford 3000™ words

1. Nawaf and Khalid showed a lot of _____ when they left their country to open a business in France.

2. We hired an architect to help us _____ our new home.

3. Mr. Gibbs is a(n) _____ on restaurant management. He has managed restaurants for 20 years and has written a book on the subject.

4. The Smiths have a strong sense of _____ in their family. They always take care of each other.

5. Our business only has six employees now, but we think it will _____ a lot over the next few years.

6. Turki's greatest _____ is his ability to keep a positive attitude when times are difficult.

7. Ford, a car company, is an extremely large _____.

8. Mr. Lee is a great teacher. I don't know how he can _____ all of those children.

B. Go online for more practice with the vocabulary.

C. **PREVIEW** Look at the images in Reading 1. What kind of business do you think the article is about? Use the chart below to think of some advantages and disadvantages of working with family members in this type of business.

Advantages	Disadvantages

Writing Tip

When you are writing, try to think of other points of view. Write your own idea, but also think about what someone else might think. Try to use some other ideas as well.

D. **QUICK WRITE** Would you open a family business? Write a short paragraph to answer the question. Use your chart from Activity C to describe the advantages and disadvantages of working in a family business. Be sure to use this section for your Unit Assignment.

Reading Skill   Skimming

Skimming is reading a text quickly to get the general idea of what it is about. Skimming is useful when you read a newspaper or magazine, read online, or take a test. When you do research, you skim an article to see if it will be useful. When you skim, use these tips.

- Read the title.
- Quickly read the first sentence of each paragraph.
- Move your eyes quickly through the text.
- Do not read every sentence or every word.
- If the text is short, read the first and last sentence of each paragraph.

A. Take one minute to skim Reading 1 on pages 103–104. As you skim, underline the first sentence of each paragraph.

B. Write what you can remember about the reading.

C. Take one minute to skim Reading 2 on pages 109–110. Then look at the chart below. Check (✓) which reading has information about each topic.

Which reading has information about...	Reading 1	Reading 2
1. a family that owned a newspaper	☐	☑
2. a restaurant business	☐	☐
3. family businesses in the United States	☐	☐
4. a family business owned by immigrants	☐	☐
5. difficulties with family businesses	☐	☐

D. Go online for more practice with skimming.

WORK WITH THE READING

A. Read the magazine article and gather information about what makes a family business successful.

Family Unity Builds Success

1   *When her five daughters were young, Helene An always told them that there was* **strength** *in* **unity***. To show this, she held up one chopstick, representing one person. Then she easily broke it into two pieces. Next, she tied several chopsticks together, representing a family. She showed the girls it was hard to break the tied chopsticks. This lesson about family unity stayed with the daughters as they grew up.*

2   Helene An and her family own a multi-million-dollar restaurant business in California. However, when Helene and her husband Danny left their home in Vietnam in 1975, they didn't have much money. They moved their family to San Francisco. There they joined Danny's mother, who owned a small Italian sandwich shop. The Ans began with only a small idea and never dreamed of the success they have today.

3   Soon after the Ans' arrival in the United States, Helene and her mother-in-law, Diana, changed the sandwich shop into a small Vietnamese restaurant. They named it Green Dragon, which symbolizes good luck in Vietnamese. The restaurant was very popular, and they **expanded** from 20 seats to 70. The five daughters helped in the restaurant when they were young. Their mother told them that they all had to work hard to reach their goals and make their family stronger. Helene did not want her daughters to always work in the family business because she thought it was too hard.

4   Eventually the girls all graduated from college and went away to work for themselves, but one by

A Vietnamese sandwich

one, the daughters returned to work in the family business. They opened new restaurants in San Francisco and in Beverly Hills, a wealthy area in Los Angeles. The daughters chose new names and styles for their restaurants. Over the years, some ideas were successful, but others were not. Even though family members sometimes disagreed with each other, they worked together to make the business successful. Daughter Elizabeth explains, "Our mother taught us that to succeed we must have unity, and to have unity we must have peace. Without the strength of the family, there is no business. So even when we don't agree, we are willing to try a new idea."

5 Their expanding business became a large **corporation** in 1996, with three generations of Ans working together. Helene is the **expert** on cooking. Helene's husband Danny An is good at making decisions. Their daughter Hannah is good with computers. Hannah's husband Danny Vu is good at thinking of new ideas and doing research. Hannah's sister Elizabeth is the family designer. She **designs** the insides of the restaurants. Their sister Monique is good at **managing**. Elizabeth says, "If you're going to work as a family, you have to know what you're good at. We work well together because we have different strengths." Even the grandchildren help out.

6 Now the Ans' corporation makes more than $20 million each year. Although they began with a small restaurant, they had big dreams, and they worked together. Now they are a big success. Helene says, "In Vietnam, I didn't have to do anything for myself. Here, I've had to do everything. But I was never unhappy because every day I could see all the members of my family, and that gave me **courage** to do more. This has been our greatest fortune[1], to work together as a family."

[1] **fortune:** good luck

B. Circle the answer to each question.

1. What is the main idea of paragraph 1?
   a. Family businesses can have problems.
   b. There is strength in working together as a family.
   c. Only family businesses are successful.

2. What is the main idea of paragraph 5?
   a. By 1996, the An family business was a large corporation.
   b. Different family members have strengths that help the business.
   c. The family members didn't know what they were good at.

3. What is the main idea of the entire article?
   a. Any family can become a big success.
   b. Family members have different strengths.
   c. A family that has unity can be successful.

C. Write the correct paragraph number next to each detail.

_____ a.   After college, the daughters returned to work in the family business.

_____ b.   The Ans' company makes more than $20 million each year.

_____ c.   Helene and Danny An left Vietnam in 1975 with little money.

_____ d.   The business became a corporation in 1996.

_____ e.   The An daughters worked in the restaurant when they were young.

D. Match each family member with the correct skill.

_e_ 1.   Helene   a. managing

_____ 2.   Danny An   b. design

_____ 3.   Hannah   c. making decisions

_____ 4.   Danny Vu   d. computers

_____ 5.   Monique   e. cooking

_____ 6.   Elizabeth   f. new ideas and research

E. Answer these questions.

1. Why didn't Helene An want her daughters to work in the family business?

   _____

2. Were all of the family's new ideas successful?

   _____

3. According to Helene An, there was one thing that the family needed for success. What was it?

   _____

4. According to Elizabeth, why do the family members work well together?

   _____

5. According to Helene An, what is the best thing about her family's situation?

   _____

F. Number these events in the order in which they occurred.

____ **a.** The business became a corporation.

____ **b.** The company made more than $20 million per year.

____ **c.** The family changed their small shop into a larger restaurant.

____ **d.** The family left their home in Vietnam without much money.

____ **e.** The family moved to San Francisco.

____ **f.** The daughters finished their education and started their own jobs.

____ **g.** The daughters came back to work with their parents.

iQ ONLINE **G. Go online to read *Who Is in Your Family?* and check your comprehension.**

WRITE WHAT YOU THINK

A. Ask and answer these questions with a partner.

1. The An family members respect each other. How does this help them have a successful business?

2. What strengths do you have that help you when working in a group?

B. Choose one of the questions and write a response. Use supporting examples. Look back at your Quick Write on page 102 as you think about what you learned.

Question: _____

My Response: _____

_____

_____

READING 2 | The Challenge of Running a Family Business

UNIT OBJECTIVE ▶▶ ▶▶

You are going to read a textbook article about the difficulties of owning a family business. Use the article to gather information and ideas for your Unit Assignment.

PREVIEW THE READING

Vocabulary Skill Review

In Unit 4, you used the dictionary to learn about pronunciation, parts of speech, and related forms of words. Use your dictionary to check on the pronunciation and related word forms of *challenge, enthusiasm, realistic,* and *responsibility*.

A. **VOCABULARY** Here are some words from Reading 2. Read the sentences. Circle the answer that best matches the meaning of each <u>underlined</u> word or phrase.

1. For many parents, communicating with their teenage children can be a big <u>challenge</u>. At this age children may not want to talk to their parents about their problems.
   a. an exciting event
   b. a difficult thing that makes you try hard

2. Mario will be a great sports reporter because of his great <u>enthusiasm</u> for sports.
   a. difficulty with something
   b. strong feeling of liking something

3. My children <u>depend on</u> me to drive them to school.
   a. need someone to provide something
   b. help someone

4. Oliver's store isn't making much money. He's worried that it's going to <u>fail</u>.
   a. be unsuccessful
   b. break the law

5. Ahmed's <u>goals</u> for the future do not include joining the family business.
   a. things that you want to do
   b. subjects that you study

6. Paula is spending more time with her friends and less time studying. Her father is worried about her change in <u>lifestyle</u>.
   a. the way that you dress
   b. the way that you live

7. My grandmother will <u>pass down</u> her jewelry to my mother.
   a. give something to a younger person
   b. create something

8. Jack still thinks he's going to become a basketball star. He needs to be more <u>realistic</u> about his career.

 a. interested and excited

 b. understanding what is possible

9. Carl's <u>responsibility</u> at home is taking out the garbage. His brother has to set the table for dinner.

 a. things that you must buy

 b. jobs or duties that you must do

10. My cousin has a <u>talent</u> for writing. She writes wonderful stories.

 a. natural skill or ability

 b. thing you want

 B. Go online for more practice with the vocabulary.

Tip for Success

When you are skimming a text, use a pencil tip to help your eyes move quickly across the text, or place a piece of paper under each line as your read. This will help you avoid stopping to read every word.

C. **PREVIEW** Skim the reading. Which paragraph gives an example of an actual family business?

D. **QUICK WRITE** What problems might owners of a family business face? Write a few sentences before you read. Be sure to use this section for your Unit Assignment.

WORK WITH THE READING

A. Read the article about the challenges of running a family business and gather information about what makes a family business successful.

The Challenge of Running a Family Business

1   In the United States, families own about 85 percent of all businesses. However, less than 30 percent of these companies last more than 20 years. The companies **fail**, and the owners can't **pass down** the family businesses to their sons and daughters. Why is it so difficult for family businesses to survive?

2   One reason may be changing times. Fifty years ago, many families owned local grocery stores. But today, small family-owned stores cannot compete with large supermarket chains. Today, most Mom and Pop stores[1] are a thing of the past[2]. The way of life is another **challenge** in a family business. A successful company requires hard work and long hours. Younger generations may not want this **lifestyle**. They may want more freedom. In addition, sons and daughters may not have the same **enthusiasm** for the business as their parents.

The Wall Street Journal

Less than 30 percent of family businesses last more than 20 years.

3   A successful family business **depends on** the family's strengths and **talents**. However, families also bring their weaknesses and personal problems to the workplace. Many families do not communicate well, and they are not good at solving problems together. These challenges often cause businesses to fail. According to Professor Randel Carlock, these problems are common. He says, "Being part of a family is very difficult. Being part of a family business is even more difficult." Love is important in a family, but love is not enough to run a family business. The business must achieve financial success.

4   The Bancroft family is an interesting example. For 105 years, the Bancroft family owned *The Wall Street Journal*. It is one of the most famous newspapers in the United States. But there were many family problems. They did not communicate well, and they disagreed about many things. One person said that they couldn't even agree on where to go for lunch! The younger family members wanted the business to be more profitable. The older members thought the quality of the paper was more important than making money. In addition, the family let people outside of

---

[1] **Mom and Pop stores:** stores owned by a family or individual, not a corporation

[2] **thing of the past:** something that no longer exists

the family manage the newspaper. They did not take part in many important decisions. Finally, in 2007, all 33 of the Bancroft family owners agreed to sell the company. Although the business had lasted several generations, the Bancrofts eventually had to sell their company because they did not manage it well. In the end, many of their family relationships suffered.

5   Many families dream of passing down their businesses to the next generation, but this requires careful planning and preparation. Good management is a key to success. All employees, especially family members, need to have clear **responsibilities**. Family business owners need to think about how decisions are made. Also, they should be **realistic** about the dreams and **goals** of the younger generation. Family businesses can be successful because of strong family ties[3]. But to succeed for more than one generation, families need to manage their businesses carefully.

[3] **ties:** something that connects you with other people

B. **Read the statements and write *T* (true) or *F* (false). Then correct each false statement to make it true.**

___ 1. Fifty percent of family businesses are passed down to the next generation.

_____

___ 2. Most family businesses change and adjust to new ideas and products.

_____

___ 3. Most owners of family businesses don't want to pass down the businesses to their sons and daughters.

_____

___ 4. According to the article, love is enough to run a family business.

_____

___ 5. The Bancroft family managed their newspaper by themselves.

_____

C. **Look back at paragraph 1 in Reading 2 to find the missing information for the sentences below.**

1. In the United States, families own about ___ percent of all businesses.

However, less than ___ percent of these businesses last more than

___ years.

2. Write each phrase from the box in the correct section of the pie charts.

> Businesses that are not family-owned
>
> Family-owned businesses
>
> Family-owned businesses that last more than 20 years
>
> Family-owned businesses that fail within 20 years

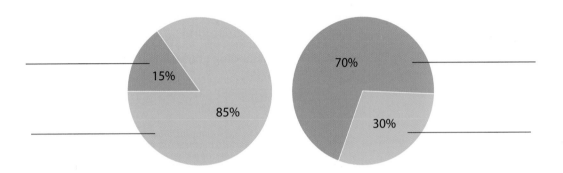

D. Look back at Reading 2 on pages 109–110 to find reasons why family businesses fail. Write two of the reasons below. Then compare your answers with a partner.

_____

_____

WRITE WHAT YOU THINK

A. Discuss these questions in a group. Look back at your Quick Write on page 108 as you think about what you learned.

1. What are some advantages to working in the same business with your family? What are some disadvantages?

2. Why do you think most small businesses fail in the first few years?

Critical Thinking **Tip**

Activity B asks you to think about a video and two articles as you answer questions. This is called **synthesizing**. When you **synthesize**, you combine ideas from several sources as you develop your own ideas.

B. Think about the unit video, Reading 1, and Reading 2 as you discuss these questions. Then choose one question and write a response.

1. What are the keys to making a family business successful?

2. What differences do you see in the three family businesses: the Feibushes (zippers), the Ans (restaurants), and the Bancrofts (newspapers)? Why do you think that the An family was successful but the Bancroft family had to sell their business?

Understanding grammatical information in the dictionary

When you look up a word in the dictionary, pay attention to the grammatical information. In addition to the part of speech, an entry may also tell you:

- if a noun is countable (C) or uncountable (U)
- if the plural of a noun has an irregular form
- if an adjective or adverb has an irregular comparative form
- if a verb has an irregular form

Looking up and understanding grammatical information about a new word helps you use the word correctly.

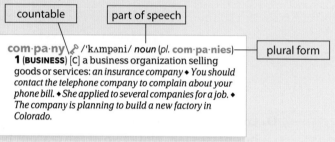

All dictionary entries are from the *Oxford American Dictionary for learners of English* © Oxford University Press 2011.

A. Use your dictionary to answer these questions.

1. Which words are uncountable? Circle them.

advantage	happiness	participant
advice	information	planet
darkness	luggage	police
furniture	news	traffic

2. What is the plural form of each of these nouns?

  a. analysis _____   c. child _____

  b. cactus _____   d. life _____

3. What is the simple past form of each of these phrases?

  a. break down _____

  b. burst into _____

  c. shine at _____

 B. Go online for more practice with using the dictionary.

WRITING

At the end of this unit, you will write a plan for a family business. This plan will include specific information from the readings and your own ideas.

Writing Skill | Unity in a paragraph

A paragraph is a group of sentences about a single idea. The topic sentence introduces the audience to the topic. The concluding sentence may summarize the contents of the paragraph. The sentences in the middle provide details to support the main idea. All of the sentences in the paragraph should be about the same main idea. The sentences should be closely related to each other. This gives the paragraph **unity**—all parts of the paragraph work together to support a single main idea.

Sentences or ideas that are <u>not</u> closely related to the main idea are irrelevant—they do not help explain and support the main idea.

To be relevant, your sentences should:

- be <u>directly</u> related to the main idea
- support the main idea, but not repeat it
- give new information or details that support the main idea
- not introduce an entirely new main idea that is different from the topic sentence

When you edit your writing, remove or change any sentences that are irrelevant. If all the sentences clearly contribute to the main idea, your paragraph will have unity.

Transition words also keep your paragraphs unified. Transition words help your paragraphs read smoothly from one sentence to the next. They help the reader see the connections between ideas. Transition words can serve several purposes:

> **to add:** *and, besides, finally, further, too, next, in addition, also, first (second, etc.)*
> **to give an example:** *for example, for instance*
> **to emphasize:** *definitely, obviously, always, certainly*

Use transition words to help keep your paragraphs unified.

A. WRITING MODEL Read the model paragraph. Then answer the questions.

Many workers today have different options about how and where they work. Thanks to technology, some people can live far away from their offices and work from home. Computers and the Internet make it possible for individuals to telecommute—that is, to use the telephone and technology to get their work done without being in the office. In addition, since most computers now have microphones and video cameras, it is easy to have a meeting even when people are far away from each other. Now if someone gets a new job, they may not have to move to a new city. Maybe in the future, no one will work in an office at all. Everyone will work from home.

1. Circle the topic sentence that has the main idea.

2. How many supporting sentences are there? Underline them.

3. Are all of the sentences in the paragraph about the same idea?

B. **WRITING MODEL** **Read the model paragraphs. Circle the main idea. Then cross out any unrelated sentences that don't help support the main idea.**

1. People from the same family are sometimes quite different. Perhaps the father is usually quiet, while the mother is likely to be noisy. Brothers and sisters can also have very different personalities. Two brothers might both be very funny. There can also be large differences in appearance. Some family members may be tall, while others are short. Perhaps they have similar hair or faces. As you can see, family members may not be very similar at all.

2. There are many keys to running a successful business. First, it is important to be sure that your business is in the right location. You want enough people to come and shop there. Many businesses fail in their first few years because they are in a poor location. A good advertising plan can also be helpful. Besides that, you must be sure that the prices are not too high or too low. If you lose money, you can borrow from a bank. My uncle did that during the first two years of his business. If you do everything right, your business can be a big success.

C. **Use the transition words from the box to complete the paragraph. For some sentences, there is more than one correct transition word.**

| finally | for instance | next |
| first | in addition | obviously |

If you want to start a new school, there are several things you must consider. _____₁, you need to think about what age group you will teach. _____₂ you must decide on the curriculum—the subject matter that you will teach.

_____₃, will your school teach driving, or will you teach photography? _____₄, you will need a place for students to study. _____₅, you will also need teachers. _____₆ you need to decide how everyone will be paid.

D. **WRITING MODEL** Read the model paragraph describing a plan for a new school. Then answer the questions.

    I am going to start a new cooking school in our neighborhood. This new school will be for college graduates who are living away from their families. In our school, we will offer classes in the morning and in the evening to fit different schedules. Also, our classes will teach the easiest and most delicious dishes. In addition, students can study specialized subjects. For example, there will be courses on making soups and on baking. The classes will be taught by experienced cooks from a variety of backgrounds. I will make sure that there are not too many students in any one class. We will get money from wealthy people and companies to help pay for the school. Finally, we will regularly ask experts to give us ideas on how to make the school better. I'm sure that our school will be popular and successful.

1. What is the main idea of the paragraph? _____

2. How many transition words do you see? _____ Circle them.

3. Do all of the ideas help support the main idea? _____

4. What are two additional ideas that the writer could add?

    _____

    _____

E. Brainstorm ideas about a plan for a special new school. What will the school be like? Who will the students be? What will you teach? It might be a school for language, photography, driving, or something else.

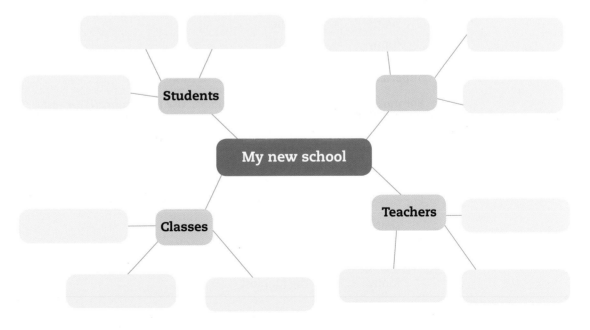

F. Write a paragraph describing a special new school. Use ideas from Activity E on page 115. Be sure you have a clear topic sentence and that all of the supporting ideas help unify the paragraph. Use transition words.

 G. Go online for more practice with paragraph unity.

Grammar	Comparative and superlative adjectives

Comparative adjectives describe the difference between two things.

For adjectives with one syllable, use **adjective + er**. *Than* often follows comparative adjectives.

tall	→	taller	The Burj Khalifa is **taller than** Taipei 101.
safe	→	safer	
big	→	bigger	

If an adjective ends in one vowel and one consonant, double the consonant, as in *big → bigger*. If the adjective ends in *-e*, just add *-r*.

For most adjectives with two or more syllables, use **more + adjective**.

| common | → | more common |
| traditional | → | more traditional |

For two-syllable adjectives that end in *-le*, add *-r*.

| simple | → | simpler |

For two-syllable adjectives that end in *-y*, change the *-y* to *i* and add *-er*.

| pretty | → | prettier |
| funny | → | funnier |

Superlative adjectives describe three or more things.

For most adjectives that have one syllable, use **the + adjective + -est**.

tall	→	the tallest
big	→	the biggest
safe	→	the safest

For two-syllable adjectives that end in *-le*, use **the** and add *–st*.

| simple | → | the simplest |

For two-syllable adjectives that end in *-y*, change the *y* to *i*, use **the**, and add *-est*.

| funny | → | the funniest |

For most adjectives with two or more syllables, add *the + most + adjective*.

informal	→	the most informal
realistic	→	the most realistic
traditional	→	the most traditional

Note: Some adjectives are irregular.

| good | → | better | → | the best |
| bad | → | worse | → | the worst |

A. Complete the paragraph with words from the box. Change them into comparative form.

| big | clear | pretty | realistic | safe | simple |

Many of us remember the good old days. Those times were

_____ and less complicated. In those days, we
                1

felt much _____ in our own neighborhoods. There
                    2

was less pollution, and the sky was _____. We
                                              3

may even feel that nature was _____ back then
                                        4

than it is now. As cities have become _____,
                                                5

those days may be gone forever. Perhaps we all need to be _____

_____ about the future.
                6

B. Look at the adjectives in the chart below. Complete the chart with the missing forms of each adjective.

Adjective	Comparative	Superlative
healthy	healthier	the healthiest
exciting		
		the closest
	easier	
	better	the best
	calmer	
busy		
	lower	

C. Complete each sentence with the correct comparative form of the adjective in parentheses.

1. I'm _____ (successful) in school than my brother is.

2. Sandra is _____ (responsible) with her money than her younger sister is.

3. Elephants are _____ (intelligent) than fish.

4. People in small towns are often _____ (friendly) than people in big cities.

5. The subway is _____ (fast) than the bus.

6. Chan's goals for the future are _____ (realistic) than Brendan's.

D. Complete each sentence with the correct superlative form of the adjective in parentheses and your own opinions. Then discuss your answers with a partner.

1. _____Ice hockey_____ is _the most interesting_ (interesting) sport to watch.

2. _____ is _____ (delicious) food in the world.

3. _____ is _____ (beautiful) season of the year.

4. _____ is _____ (difficult) sport to play.

5. _____ is _____ (famous) place in my country.

6. _____ is _____ (successful) company in the world.

E. Go online for more practice with comparative and superlative adjectives.

F. Go online for the grammar expansion.

UNIT OBJECTIVE

In this assignment, you will write a plan for a new family business. Your plan will include information about your new business, the services it will provide, and the jobs that the members of your family will do. As you prepare to write your plan, think about the Unit Question, "What makes a family business successful?" Use information from Reading 1, Reading 2, the unit video, and your work in the unit to support your writing. Refer to the Self-Assessment checklist on page 120.

iQ ONLINE

Go to the Online Writing Tutor for a writing model and alternate Unit Assignments.

PLAN AND WRITE

A. **BRAINSTORM** Freewrite to brainstorm ideas for your new family business. What are some possible businesses? What items will you sell or what services will you provide? Think about what jobs the members of your family will do. Write down as many ideas as you can.

_____

_____

_____

_____

_____

Writing **Tip**

When you are writing a plan, don't just think about what you would like to see. Think about your audience. What might readers want to know about your business?

B. **PLAN** Review your freewriting. Choose the business you want to write about. Then answer the questions.

1. What kind of business will it be? What kind of product or service will your business provide?

2. Describe the store or service.

3. Who will your customers be?

4. Why will your business be different from others?

5. Which family members will work in your company? What will their jobs be?

6. Why should people come and buy from your company?

7. Why will your business be successful?

C. **WRITE** Use your **PLAN** notes to write your plan for a new family business. Go to *iQ Online* to use the Online Writing Tutor.

1. Write your topic sentence first. Make sure the topic sentence introduces the main idea of the paragraph.

2. Be sure to use examples to support your main idea.

3. Be sure that each sentence is relevant and contributes to the main idea.

4. Look at the Self-Assessment checklist to guide your writing.

REVISE AND EDIT

 A. **PEER REVIEW** Read your partner's plan. Then go online and use the Peer Review worksheet. Discuss the review with your partner.

B. **REWRITE** Based on your partner's review, revise and rewrite your plan.

C. **EDIT** Complete the Self-Assessment checklist as you prepare to write the final draft of your plan. Be prepared to hand in your work or discuss it in class.

SELF-ASSESSMENT		
Yes	**No**	
☐	☐	Do the sentences in your paragraph support the topic sentence?
☐	☐	Do you use transition words to unify the plan and help your ideas flow smoothly?
☐	☐	Underline any comparative or superlative adjectives. Are they in the correct form?
☐	☐	Is each word used correctly? Check a dictionary if you are not sure.
☐	☐	Does the plan include vocabulary from the unit?
☐	☐	Did you check the plan for punctuation, spelling, and grammar.

 D. **REFLECT** Go to the Online Discussion Board to discuss these questions.

1. What is something new you learned in this unit?

2. Look back at the Unit Question—What makes a family business successful? Is your answer different now than when you started the unit? If yes, how is it different? Why?

TRACK YOUR SUCCESS

Circle the words and phrases you have learned in this unit.

Nouns
challenge 🔑 AWL
corporation AWL
courage 🔑
enthusiasm 🔑
expert 🔑 AWL
goal 🔑 AWL
lifestyle
responsibility 🔑

strength 🔑
talent 🔑
unity

Verbs
design 🔑 AWL
expand 🔑 AWL
fail 🔑
manage 🔑

Adjectives
realistic 🔑

Phrasal Verbs
depend on 🔑
pass down

🔑 Oxford 3000™ words
AWL Academic Word List

Check (✓) the skills you learned. If you need more work on a skill, refer to the page(s) in parentheses.

READING ■	I can skim. (p. 102)
VOCABULARY ■	I can use the dictionary to understand grammatical information. (p. 112)
WRITING ■	I can write a paragraph with unified ideas. (p. 113)
GRAMMAR ■	I can use comparative and superlative adjectives correctly. (pp. 116–117)
UNIT OBJECTIVE ▶▶▶▶ ■	I can gather information and ideas to write a plan for a new family business.

READING ▶ identifying the author's purpose
VOCABULARY ▶ using the dictionary
WRITING ▶ describing a process
GRAMMAR ▶ infinitives of purpose

UNIT QUESTION

Do you prefer to get help from a person or a machine?

A Discuss these questions with your classmates.

1. What are some of the advantages of getting help from a machine rather than from a person?

2. What are some of the advantages of getting help from a person rather than a machine?

3. Look at the photo. What are the men doing?

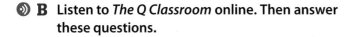

B Listen to *The Q Classroom* online. Then answer these questions.

1. Which students prefer to get help from people? Which machines do they dislike?

2. Which students prefer to get help from machines? Which machines do they like?

3. Think of one of the machines that the students mentioned in their discussion. Do you like using that type of machine or technology? Why or why not?

iQ ONLINE **C** Go online to watch the video about technology in a restaurant. Then check your comprehension.

VIDEO VOCABULARY

customize *(v.)* to change something to suit the needs of the owner

fusion *(adj.)* cooking that is a mixture of different styles

hover *(v.)* to wait near someone in an uncertain manner

virtual *(adj.)* made to appear to exist with the use of computer software

iQ ONLINE **D** Go to the Online Discussion Board to discuss the Unit Question with your classmates.

E **Look at the photos and answer the questions with a partner.**

a

Touch-screen ordering kiosk

b

Airport check-in kiosk

c

Supermarket self-service check-out

d

Gas station self-service pump kiosk

1. Which of these self-service machines have you used?

2. How does each of these self-service machines save time?

3. What problems could you have with each machine?

4. Which machine is the most useful? The least useful?

F **Discuss these questions with your classmates.**

1. How many classmates have used each machine in Activity E?

2. What other self-service machines do you and your classmates sometimes use?

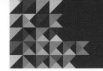
READING 1 | Memo to Restaurant Servers

UNIT OBJECTIVE ▶▶▶▶

You are going to read a business memo from a restaurant manager to the servers. Use the memo to gather information and ideas for your Unit Assignment.

Vocabulary Skill Review

In Unit 4, you learned to use the dictionary to find additional information about words. Look up the words *benefit* and *blame*. Which prepositions are often used with these words? Which prepositions are used with them if you change the part of speech?

PREVIEW THE READING

A. **VOCABULARY** Here are some words from Reading 1. Read their definitions. Then complete each sentence.

> **automatically** (*adverb*) 🔑 done in a way (like a machine) that does not require human control
>
> **benefit** (*noun*) 🔑 advantages or good or useful effects of something
>
> **blame** (*verb*) 🔑 to think or say that someone is responsible for something bad that happened
>
> **decrease** (*verb*) 🔑 to become or to make something smaller or less
>
> **error** (*noun*) 🔑 a mistake
>
> **estimate** (*verb*) 🔑 to calculate the approximate size, cost, or amount of something
>
> **interact** (*verb*) to communicate or mix with
>
> **provide** (*verb*) 🔑 to give or supply something to somebody
>
> **stressed** (*adjective*) 🔑 feeling worried or unable to relax
>
> **unique** (*adjective*) 🔑 unlike anything else; being the only one of its type

🔑 Oxford 3000™ words

1. A _____ of having a laptop computer is that you can use it almost anywhere.

2. At the bank, a machine _____ sorts and counts coins.

3. I thought I made many mistakes on the test, but later I found out that I had made only one _____.

4. I am waiting for prices to _____ before I buy a new laptop.

5. Some people _____ the changes in climate on pollution.

6. I _____ that 50 people will be at the meeting?

7. My brother is good with children. He likes to _____ with them.

8. Last year I felt very _____ about my schoolwork. This year, I have fewer classes, and I feel more relaxed.

9. The school librarians are very helpful. They _____ us with a lot of useful information.

10. Instead of a typical cake, Sue made a _____ and colorful one.

B. Go online for more practice with the vocabulary.

Tip for Success

Before you read a text, look at the title, photos, and format of the text. Think about what kind of information it might contain.

C. **PREVIEW** Quickly read the topic of the memo (in the RE: line) and the questions in paragraph 4 of the memo. What do you think the new technology will be in the restaurant? More than one answer is possible.

☐ Customers will pay their own bills using a credit card at a tablet.

☐ Customers will enter their order at their table using a tablet.

☐ Customers will use their cell phones to order at their table.

D. **QUICK WRITE** Think of three ways that restaurants use technology. How is each way useful? How does it make dining more enjoyable for customers? Write your response before you read the article. Be sure to use this section for your Unit Assignment.

WORK WITH THE READING

A. Read the business memo and gather information about getting help from a machine.

Restaurant Z   Memo

DATE: May 3
TO: Servers
FROM: Mark McCormick, Dining Room Manager
RE: New touch-screen ordering

1   At Restaurant Z, we are known as a cool, trendy place for people who want a special experience. We are always looking for better ways to serve our customers and make their experience **unique**. Next month, we will make

a change so that we can really stand out[1]: touch-screen ordering, also known as "digital dining." You need to know about this new technology.

2   This is how it works: Each table will have its own tablet with a touch screen. Customers can view the menu on the tablet, including descriptions and photos. To start, the customer swipes her credit card and puts in her order by touching the screen. Then the program **automatically** makes suggestions for additional items to order, such as appetizers[2] and drinks. When the customer is ready, she pushes a button to send the order directly to the computer in the kitchen. Won't that make your job as a server easier? All you have to do is bring the food to the table when it's ready! Finally, paying the bill is quick and easy because the customer can do it herself. This exciting new technology will improve our customers' dining experience and increase your tips!

3   Now you may want to know how this change will affect you. Maybe you are afraid of losing your job. Let me assure you: you won't. In fact, you will be able to serve more customers every night! These high-tech tablets not only look cool, they **decrease** the number of tasks you have to do! Hopefully, that means that you can serve more tables without feeling **stressed**.

4   Here are some questions and answers:

Q: *What are the **benefits** for me as a server?*

A: First of all, with digital dining, customers can order quickly. We will be able to serve more customers in less time. Also, the tablet program will automatically suggest additional items to order. Research shows that when this happens, customers order more. We **estimate** that customer bills will be 15 to 20 percent higher. With more customers ordering more items, you will earn more money in tips. In addition, you won't have to repeat the same information over and over like a robot[3]. Finally, customers can't **blame** you for **errors** in their order—they place their own orders!

Q: *Will customers really want to do their own ordering?*

A: Yes, I think that most of our customers will love it! If a diner prefers the traditional service, we will **provide** it. But these tablets will be so much fun that everyone will want to use them! The photographs will be fantastic and the descriptions will be mouth-watering. As you know, most of our customers are tech-savvy[4], and they enjoy **interacting** with the latest gadgets[5].

---

[1] **stand out:** to be different
[2] **appetizer:** a small amount of food that you eat as the first part of a meal
[3] **robot:** an automated machine that can do work that a person does
[4] **tech-savvy:** having knowledge and understanding of technology
[5] **gadget:** a small machine or tool

Q: *What other features will these tablets have?*

A: They'll have entertaining games and high-speed Internet access. Customers can send messages to friends and post photos of themselves at the table.

5 We will be having an employee training session to show you how digital dining works next Tuesday from 9:30–11:00 a.m. I look forward to showing you this fabulous new system!

B. Circle the answer to each question.

1. What is the main reason the restaurant is going to use digital dining?
   a. to provide better service to customers
   b. to help servers get larger tips
   c. to be trendy and popular

2. What was the manager's reason for writing the second section?
   a. to tell how digital dining will increase sales
   b. to explain how digital dining works
   c. to describe how customers will pay their bills

3. Why does the manager include the question and answer section?
   a. to explain the training servers will receive
   b. to answer questions that customer will ask
   c. to answer questions that servers will have

4. What is the main idea of the question and answer section?
   a. Someday tablets will replace servers.
   b. Tablets will make servers and customers happy.
   c. Customers will order more food.

C. Complete each statement with information from the memo.

1. The date of the memo is _____.

2. The restaurant will start using tablets _____.

3. In addition to descriptions of menu items, the tablet will show

   _____.

4. When a customer places an order, the tablet program will recommend

   _____.

5. Customers' bills will be _____ when they use digital dining.

6. The training meeting will be _____.

D. Complete the sentences to show the causes and effects or results. Use information from the reading.

Cause		Effect or result
1. Because the tablet will do many of the servers' tasks,	→	<u>servers will feel less stressed.</u> _____
2. _____ _____	→	servers will make more money.
3. _____ _____	→	customers cannot blame servers for mistakes in their orders.
4. Because the tablet automatically suggests other items to order,	→	_____ _____
5. Because the tablets will be so much fun to use,	→	_____ _____

E. Answer these questions.

1. Why does the manager use *we* and *our* in section 1?
   a. because the servers own the restaurant, too
   b. because he wants the servers to feel they are part of a team
   c. because he is also a server

2. Find and underline other uses of *we* and *our* in the memo.

   What sections are they in? _____

3. In section 2, the manager asks, "Won't that make your job as a server easier?" Why does he ask this question?

a. because he is not sure if the servers will agree with him

b. because he doesn't know what the servers' answers will be

c. because he expects the servers to agree with him

4. Which sentence from the memo expresses enthusiasm and excitement for this change?

a. "You need to know about this new technology."

b. "This exciting new technology will improve our customer's dining experience and increase your tips!"

c. "Maybe you are afraid of losing your job."

5. Find and underline another sentence that expresses enthusiasm. What

section is it in? _____

 F. Go online to read *Voice Recognition Systems* and check your comprehension.

 ## WRITE WHAT YOU THINK

A. Discuss these questions in a group.

1. The manager mentions many of the benefits of the new tablets. What do you think some of the disadvantages or problems might be?

2. At Restaurant Z, who do you think will benefit the most from the new digital dining technology: the customers or the servers?

3. Have you ever used technology like this in a restaurant? If so, describe your experience and tell what happened. If not, would you like to use this technology? Why or why not?

B. Choose one of the questions and write a response. Look back at your Quick Write on page 126 as you think about what you learned.

Question: _____

My Response: _____

_____

_____

_____

The **purpose** of a text is the reason the author writes it. For example, the purpose of a newspaper article is to inform or give the reader information about something. The purpose of a letter to the newspaper is usually to express an opinion about something. As you read, look at the words the author uses and ask yourself questions to help you identify the purpose. Here are some questions you can ask yourself as you read:

- Is the author trying to give me information about something?
- Is the author expressing his or her opinion about something?
- Is the author telling me a personal story?
- Is the author trying to make me interested or excited about something?
- Is the author trying to make me laugh?

Identifying the author's purpose can help you better understand the text you are reading.

A. Look back at Reading 1 on pages 126–128. What is the author's purpose? Circle two answers.

a. to tell a story

b. to make someone laugh

c. to give information

d. to make someone excited about something

B. Read the titles. Look at the words the authors use. Then match each title with the correct purpose.

____ 1. "My Embarrassing Adventures with Technology"   a. to tell a story

____ 2. "Competitive Sports Are Too Competitive"   b. to make someone laugh

____ 3. "My Grandfather's Childhood in Egypt"   c. to express an opinion

____ 4. "New Research Shows Birds See More Colors"   d. to make someone interested in something

____ 5. "You Can Be Stronger in Two Weeks!"   e. to give information

 C. Go online for more practice with identifying the author's purpose.

READING 2 | I Hate Machines!

 You are going to read a blog about how technology can cause problems. A blog is a website with posts or short essays. Use the blog to gather information and ideas for your Unit Assignment.

PREVIEW THE READING

Vocabulary Skill Review

In Unit 5, you learned about grammatical information in the dictionary. Look at the vocabulary on this page and on page 125. Using a dictionary, find out which nouns are countable, which are uncountable, and which can be either countable or uncountable.

A. **VOCABULARY** Here are some words from Reading 2. Read their definitions. Then complete each sentence.

---

access (*noun*) 🔑 a way to enter a place or to use something

assist (*verb*) 🔑 to help someone

connection (*noun*) 🔑 a path of communication for a telephone or Internet

eventually (*adverb*) 🔑 after a long time

frustrated (*adjective*) angry or impatient because you cannot do or achieve what you want to do

furious (*adjective*) very angry

install (*verb*) 🔑 to put a new thing in its place so it is ready to use

on hold (*prepositional phrase*) waiting on the phone to talk to someone or continue a conversation

scan (*verb*) to pass light over a picture or document in order to copy it and put it in the memory of a computer

transfer (*verb*) 🔑 to connect a telephone caller to another person or line

---

🔑 Oxford 3000™ words

1. I thought my friends would never come back from the store, but

    _____ they did.

2. Ana called, but I couldn't hear her because my phone had a bad

    _____.

3. This key will give you _____ to my apartment whenever

    you want.

4. At our store the computer specialists _____ customers.

    It's their job.

5. I'm not able to answer your question, but I can _____ you

    to a manager who can help you.

6. You don't need to type the price into the cash register. You can just

    _____ the item with this machine.

7. I tried to register for classes today, but the website didn't work! Now all the classes I want are full. I'm so _____.

8. I hung up after I was _____ for 30 minutes.

9. My friend damaged my new car, and then he lied to me about what happened. I was _____!

10. A man came to my apartment to _____ my new dishwasher.

 B. Go online for more practice with the vocabulary.

C. **PREVIEW** Blogs are usually informal and personal. Bloggers, people who create blogs, often write about their experiences, giving their opinions about various topics. Look at the title of the blog post in Reading 2. What do you think the reading will be about?

D. **QUICK WRITE** Think about the title, "I Hate Machines!" Think about an experience you had with a machine that made you feel the same way. What happened? Write a few sentences about the topic. Be sure to use this section for your Unit Assignment.

WORK WITH THE READING

A. Read the blog and gather information about getting help from a machine.

I Hate Machines!

Home   Log in

Trouble with Technology

About

TUESDAY, MARCH 2

Links

1   Recently, I moved to a new apartment right across the street from my old one. I thought it would be simple to get my phone and DSL[1] line started. The technician[2] from the phone company came to **install** my telephone line. He said that I would be able to use the Internet on the same line. After he left, I discovered that the phone worked, but the DSL

Archives

January

February

March

---

[1] **DSL:** a fast Internet connection through telephone lines. The letters stand for digital subscriber line.   [2] **technician:** a person who fixes machines

April
May
June
July
August
September
October
November
December

connection for the Internet didn't. So I called the phone company. Of course, I didn't get to talk to a real person. Instead, an automated voice recording asked me a lot of questions. Then I had to wait for half an hour to talk to a real person. While I was **on hold**, every few minutes a recording said, "Remember, you can use our convenient website to solve most of your problems." "Arrrrrghh!!" I said to the recording, feeling **frustrated.** "Why do you think I'm calling you? I don't have a connection to the Internet."

2   I finally got to talk to a real person, but then she **transferred** me back into the automated system again. I couldn't get any help. I called a different number, and the person told me to be at my house for a technician to come the next day. I stayed home from work, but nobody came! I called them again. The recording said, "We're sorry, all agents are busy **assisting** other customers. We are unable to take your call." Then the machine hung up on me. Three days later, I received a phone call from them. But again, it wasn't a real person: it was a machine. The voice on the machine said, "We are happy to tell you that you now have Internet **access**." But when I went back to my computer, I still couldn't connect to the Internet. I was **furious**!

3   To make a long story short[3], it took the phone company two weeks to solve my problem. I spent a total of 18 hours at home waiting for workers who never came. I spent eight hours on the phone listening to recordings and machines and waiting on hold. Companies think that these voice-activated systems save us time, but they actually waste it.

4   The telephone isn't the only timesaving technology that drives me crazy[4]. The other day, I went to the supermarket. They had a new self-service checkout system. With this new device, I could **scan** my groceries myself instead of waiting in a checkout line. For some strange reason, these machines seem to hate me. Here's what happened: I scan my item. The computer sits there stupidly and does nothing. **Eventually** it says, "Scan your first item." But I already did! What do I do now? Scan it again and get charged twice? So I put my item in the bag.

5   "Put the item in the bag," says the machine. But I already have!

6   "Put the item in the bag," it says again. So, I take it out and do it again, just to make the machine happy.

7   "Scan the item before putting it in the bag!" shouts the machine while everyone turns to look at me as if I'm an idiot[5]. Grrr!

8   I wish we could go back to the good old days when there were real people to help us. I think I would have been happier living a hundred years ago, before we had all of this timesaving, self-service technology.

---

[3] **to make a long story short:** to tell something quickly

[4] **drive me crazy:** to make me upset or angry

[5] **as if I'm an idiot:** as if they think that I am stupid

B. Answer these questions.

1. What are the two types of automated technology with which the author was frustrated?

   _____

2. What was frustrating about his first experience? List three things.

   _____

3. How did he feel when he used the self-service checkout? Why?

   _____

4. Why does the writer hate machines? Give at least three reasons.

   _____

5. What is the author's purpose? (Look back at the reading skill on page 131.)

   _____

6. The blog is humorous. In your opinion, what was the funniest part?

   _____

C. Read the statements. Write *T* (true) or *F* (false). Then correct each false statement to make it true.

____ 1. A worker went to the man's house to install a phone line.

   _____

____ 2. When the man called the telephone company, he never got to talk to a real person.

   _____

____ 3. It took the phone company three weeks to solve his problem.

   _____

____ 4. The computer at the supermarket did not work correctly.

   _____

____ 5. The man thinks he would prefer to have lived in a time before there was technology.

   _____

D. Look at Reading 2. Identify who said each of the statements. Write *P* if it was a person. Write *C* if it was a computer or an automated voice.

___ 1. "Remember, you can use our convenient website to solve most of your problems."

___ 2. "Arrrrrghh!!"

___ 3. "Why do you think I'm calling you?"

___ 4. "We're sorry, all agents are busy assisting other customers."

___ 5. "Scan the item before putting it in the bag!"

E. Read the statements. Number them to show the correct order.

___ a. I discovered that the phone worked, but the Internet connection didn't.

___ b. The person transferred me to the automated system again.

___ c. A technician from the phone company installed a phone line.

___ d. After two weeks, I finally got my Internet connection.

___ e. I made an appointment, but no one came to fix the connection.

___ f. I called the phone company, waited on hold, and finally spoke with a real person.

WRITE WHAT YOU THINK

A. Discuss these questions in a group. Look back at your Quick Write on page 133 as you think about what you learned.

1. Have you ever been frustrated by new technology? Describe what happened.

2. Do you prefer to interact with people or with self-service machines? Why?

Writing **Tip**

When you write a paragraph in response to a question, begin with a topic sentence. Support your ideas with reasons, supporting details, and examples. End with a strong concluding sentence.

B. Think about the unit video, Reading 1, and Reading 2 as you discuss these questions. Then choose one question and write a response.

1. Think of a new type of self-service technology. What are the disadvantages or problems?

2. What is your favorite type of self-service technology? Describe what it is and why you like it.

Words with more than one meaning

Many words have more than one meaning, or definition, even if they are spelled and pronounced the same way. Using a dictionary can help you identify the correct meaning of a new word. If a word has two definitions that are the same part of speech (*noun, verb, adjective, adverb*), they will likely appear under the same entry in the dictionary. If the two meanings are different parts of speech, they might appear under different entries in the dictionary.

light¹ /laɪt/ *noun* **1** [C, U] the energy from the sun, a lamp, etc. that allows you to see things: *a beam/ray of light* ◆ *the light of the sun* ◆ *The light was too bad for us to read by.* **2** [C] something that produces light, for example an electric lamp: *Suddenly, all the lights came on/went out.* ◆ *the lights of the city in the distance* ◆ *a neon light* ◆ *That car's lights aren't on.* ◆ *Please switch the lights off before you leave.*

light² /laɪt/ *adj.*
> **NOT DARK 1** having a lot of light: *In the summer it's still light at 9 o'clock.* ◆ *a light room* **ANT dark**
> **OF A COLOR 2** pale in color: *a light blue sweater* **ANT dark**
> **NOT HEAVY 3** not of great weight: *Carry this bag – it's the lightest.* ◆ *I've lost weight – I'm five pounds lighter than I used to be.* ◆ *light clothes* (= for summer) **ANT heavy**

You can improve your vocabulary by using a dictionary to look up words with more than one meaning.

All dictionary entries are from the *Oxford American Dictionary for learners of English* © Oxford University Press 2011.

A. Use your dictionary to find the different definitions of the words below. Then write the definition and the sentence that uses the word in context. Compare your answers with a partner.

1. light

    Definition 1: _the energy from the sun, a lamp, etc._

    Sentence: _The light was too low for us to see._

    Definition 2: _something that produces light, for example an electric lamp_

    Sentence: _Suddenly, all the lights came on._

    Definition 3: _____

    Sentence: _____

    Definition 4: _____

    Sentence: _____

Rowing

2. row

Definition 1: _____

Sentence: _____

Definition 2: _____

Sentence: _____

3. tip

Definition 1: _____

Sentence: _____

Definition 2: _____

Sentence: _____

Definition 3: _____

Sentence: _____

4. bank

Definition 1: _____

Sentence: _____

Definition 2: _____

Sentence: _____

Definition 3: _____

Sentence: _____

(Tip) **for Success**

Sometimes words with more than one meaning are spelled the same way, but they are pronounced differently. Pay attention to the different pronunciations for the different meanings of *record* and *wind*.

B. **Work with a partner. Look up the words *record* and *wind* in the dictionary. Answer the questions below.**

1. How many definitions are there for the word *record*? ____

2. How many of the definitions did you already know? ____

3. How many definitions are there for the word *wind*? ____

4. How many of the definitions did you already know? ____

 C. **Go online for more practice with using the dictionary.**

WRITING

UNIT OBJECTIVE ▶▶▶

At the end of this unit, you will write a paragraph describing the steps of a process performed by either a person or a machine. This paragraph will include specific information from the readings and your own ideas.

Writing Skill | Describing a process

When you write about a **process**, you describe how to do something step-by-step. First, you write a topic sentence that states what the process is. Then you explain each step clearly. Use **time order** words to help guide your reader. Time order words usually come at the beginning of a sentence and are followed by a comma. Note that *then* is not followed by a comma.

Tip for Success

Use several different time order words in your writing. This will help make your writing more interesting to the reader.

first	next	then	later	after that	finally

First, turn on your computer.
Then go to our website.

Use these time order words to link two steps in a process.

after	as soon as	before	when	while

Before you download the program, read the directions.
While the program is downloading, you can check your email.

A. **WRITING MODEL** Read the model instructions for digital dining. Circle the time order words.

    Digital dining is an easy way to order food. First, view the menu on your tabletop monitor. Then insert your credit card. Next, use the touch screen to enter your order. When you're ready, push the button to send your order. While you wait for your food, you can take photos and send them to your friends. Finally, use the monitor to pay your bill with a credit card.

Using an ATM

B. Read the steps about how to use an ATM (automated teller machine). Then write the steps in the flow chart on page 140 to show the correct order.

a. Press "withdraw."

b. Insert your ATM card.

c. Push "done."

d. Read the choices.

e. Remove the money from the slot.

f. Enter your PIN (personal identification number).

g. Enter the amount of money.

h. Take your receipt and your card.

Process: How to use an ATM

Start

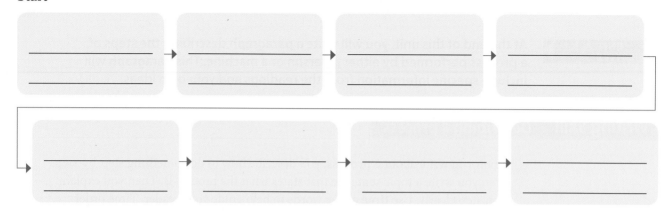

Finish

C. Write the process from Activity B in a paragraph, using time order words. You may combine two steps into one sentence.

D. Think of a process that describes something that you know how to make, fix, or use. Then write notes for the steps in the flow chart. Add more boxes if you need to.

Process: _____

Start

Finish

E. Show your flow chart to a partner and explain the steps. Answer any questions about the process. Do you need to add additional steps or information? Add notes to your chart.

F. What are some things that sometimes go wrong in your process? What are some extra tips you can include? Complete the sentences on page 141 to give additional information about the process.

1. When you _____, be sure that you

   _____.

2. Be careful when you _____ because sometimes

   _____.

3. Don't forget to _____. You will

   _____ if you don't _____.

G. Use your flow chart and one or two sentences from activity F to write a paragraph describing a process. Make sure to use time order words.

 H. Go online for more practice with describing a process.

An **infinitive** is *to* + the base form of a verb. We sometimes use infinitives to show the purpose of an action. We call these **infinitives of purpose**. An infinitive of purpose is usually separated from the main verb in a sentence. Infinitives of purpose can be used with most action verbs.

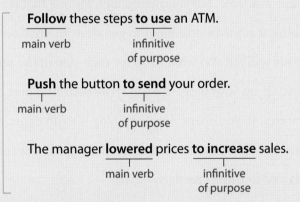

Follow these steps **to use** an ATM.
— main verb   — infinitive of purpose

Push the button **to send** your order.
— main verb   — infinitive of purpose

The manager **lowered** prices **to increase** sales.
— main verb   — infinitive of purpose

Sometimes an infinitive of purpose comes before the main verb.

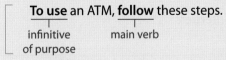

To use an ATM, **follow** these steps.
— infinitive of purpose   — main verb

Not all infinitives are infinitives of purpose. An infinitive of purpose has the same meaning as *in order to*. If you insert the phrase *in order to*, it will help you figure out if an infinitive is one that shows purpose.

Infinitive of purpose:

⌈ He called me **to apologize.**
⌊ He called me **in order to apologize.** (same meaning)

Not an infinitive of purpose:

⌈ He called me and said that he wanted **to apologize.**
⌊ He called me and said that he wanted **in order to apologize.** (not the same
    meaning and incorrect)

A. Circle each infinitive of purpose in the paragraph. Remember, not every infinitive shows purpose.

Creating your own online blog is a good way to connect with people who share your interests. I started a blog last year (to share) my experience as an international exchange student in Miami, Florida. It was very easy to do, and it allowed me to practice my writing skills and be in touch with other students. Here's how you do it. First, go online to find free blog websites. There are many available, but you should look for one that is easy to use. Start by looking at some sample blogs to get ideas for your own blog. Then get started! The site will tell you what to do for each step of the set-up process. After you have set up your blog, you can write your first post. Use photos to add visual interest to your page. Having a blog is a fun experience because you get comments from people who read it. It's also a great way to practice your writing skills and to think creatively.

B. Answer these questions using infinitives of purpose.

1. Why do you use the Internet?

   _____

2. What is another kind of technology that you use? Why do you use it?

   _____

3. Why do companies use voice-automated telephone systems?

   _____

4. Why are you studying English?

_____

C. Go online for more practice with infinitives of purpose.

D. Go online for the grammar expansion.

Unit Assignment | Write a paragraph describing a process

UNIT OBJECTIVE ▶▶▶▶ **In this assignment, you will write a paragraph describing a process done by either a person or a machine. As you prepare your paragraph, think about the Unit Question, "Do you prefer to get help from a person or a machine?" Use information from Reading 1, Reading 2, the unit video, and your work in this unit to support your paragraph. Refer to the Self-Assessment checklist on page 144.**

Go to the Online Writing Tutor for a writing model and alternate Unit Assignments.

PLAN AND WRITE

A. BRAINSTORM Use the chart to brainstorm ideas for a topic. Then share your ideas with a partner. Decide which topics are the most interesting.

Self-service technology and machines	Things I can make by myself	Things I can repair by myself

Critical Thinking **Tip**

In Activity B you **identify** the steps in a process. To describe a process, you have to break the process down into separate steps. **Identifying** the steps or parts of a process helps you to understand it better.

B. PLAN Complete the activities.

1. Look at your chart in Activity A and select a topic for your paragraph.

2. Think about how you will explain the steps of the process. Make a flow chart of the steps in order. Then make a list of time order words you can use to connect the steps of your process.

C. **WRITE** Use your **PLAN** notes to write your paragraph. Go to *iQ Online* to use the Online Writing Tutor.

1. Write a topic sentence for your paragraph. Then use your notes from Activity B to write your paragraph. Use time order words from the Writing Skill on page 139. Use infinitives of purpose where you can. Include sentences with additional tips and information about what can go wrong.

2. Look at the Self-Assessment checklist to guide your writing.

REVISE AND EDIT

A. **PEER REVIEW** Read a partner's paragraph. Then go online and use the Peer Review worksheet. Discuss the review with your partner.

B. **REWRITE** Based on your partner's review, revise and rewrite your paragraph.

C. **EDIT** Complete the Self-Assessment checklist as you prepare to write the final draft of your paragraph. Be prepared to hand in your work or discuss it in class.

Yes	No	SELF-ASSESSMENT
☐	☐	Do you describe the process clearly using time order words?
☐	☐	Does your paragraph include infinitives of purpose?
☐	☐	Is each word spelled correctly? Check a dictionary if you are not sure.
☐	☐	Does the paragraph include vocabulary from the unit?
☐	☐	Did you check the paragraph for punctuation, spelling, and grammar?

D. **REFLECT** Go to the Online Discussion Board to discuss these questions.

1. What is something new you learned in this unit?

2. Look back at the Unit Question—Do you prefer to get help from a person or a machine? Is your answer different now than when you started the unit? If yes, how is it different? Why?

TRACK YOUR SUCCESS

Circle the words and phrases you have learned in this unit.

Nouns
access 🔑 AWL
benefit 🔑 AWL
connection 🔑
error 🔑 AWL

Verbs
assist 🔑 AWL
blame 🔑
decrease 🔑
estimate 🔑 AWL
install 🔑

interact AWL
provide 🔑
scan
transfer 🔑 AWL

Adjectives
frustrated
furious
stressed 🔑 AWL
unique 🔑 AWL

Adverbs
automatically 🔑 AWL
eventually 🔑 AWL

Phrases
on hold

🔑 Oxford 3000™ words
AWL Academic Word List

Check (✓) the skills you learned. If you need more work on a skill, refer to the page(s) in parentheses.

READING	■	I can identify the author's purpose. (p. 131)
VOCABULARY	■	I can use the dictionary to identify the correct meanings of words. (p. 137)
WRITING	■	I can describe a step-by-step process. (p. 139)
GRAMMAR	■	I can use infinitives of purpose correctly. (pp. 141–142)
UNIT OBJECTIVE ▶▶▶▶	■	I can gather information and ideas to write a paragraph describing the steps of a process.

UNIT **7**

READING ▶ identifying fact and opinion
VOCABULARY ▶ phrasal verbs
WRITING ▶ using sentence variety
GRAMMAR ▶ simple past and past continuous

Environmental Studies

UNIT QUESTION

Is it better to save what you have or buy new things?

A Discuss these questions with your classmates.

1. What are some things that people choose to have repaired when they are broken?

2. What is the oldest piece of clothing that you still wear? How old is it? Why do you still have it?

3. Look at the photo. Do you buy things when they go on sale?

B Listen to *The Q Classroom* online. Then answer these questions.

1. Marcus says that old things become outdated. What does he mean?

2. Una says that that buying new things is good for the economy. What does she mean? Do you agree?

 C Go to the Online Discussion Board to discuss the Unit Question with your classmates.

ADDITIONAL
50% OFF
ALL MARKDOWNS

SELECT ITEMS ONLY

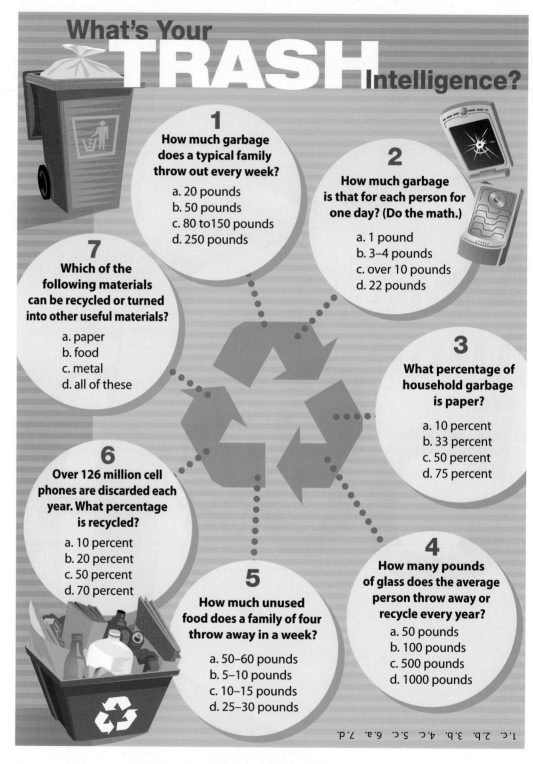

D Look at the quiz below. Answer the questions about garbage.

What's Your TRASH Intelligence?

1 How much garbage does a typical family throw out every week?
a. 20 pounds
b. 50 pounds
c. 80 to150 pounds
d. 250 pounds

2 How much garbage is that for each person for one day? (Do the math.)
a. 1 pound
b. 3–4 pounds
c. over 10 pounds
d. 22 pounds

3 What percentage of household garbage is paper?
a. 10 percent
b. 33 percent
c. 50 percent
d. 75 percent

4 How many pounds of glass does the average person throw away or recycle every year?
a. 50 pounds
b. 100 pounds
c. 500 pounds
d. 1000 pounds

5 How much unused food does a family of four throw away in a week?
a. 50–60 pounds
b. 5–10 pounds
c. 10–15 pounds
d. 25–30 pounds

6 Over 126 million cell phones are discarded each year. What percentage is recycled?
a. 10 percent
b. 20 percent
c. 50 percent
d. 70 percent

7 Which of the following materials can be recycled or turned into other useful materials?
a. paper
b. food
c. metal
d. all of these

1.c. 2.b. 3.b. 4.c. 5.c. 6.a. 7.d.

E Discuss your answers with a partner. Then look at the answers at the bottom of the quiz. How many did you get correct? Did any answers surprise you?

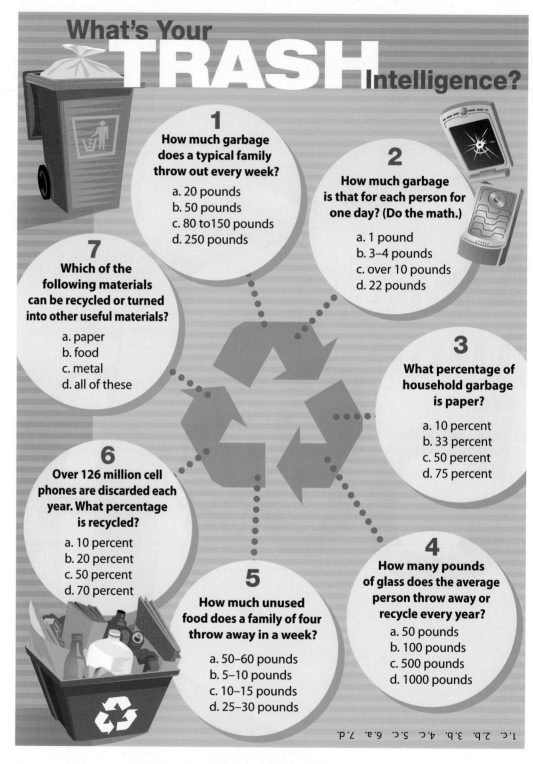

READING

READING 1 | Think Before You Toss

You are going to read a magazine article about why we should keep things instead of throwing them away. Use the article to gather information and ideas for your Unit Assignment.

PREVIEW THE READING

Vocabulary Skill Review

In Unit 6, you learned to use the dictionary to find the definition of words with more than one meaning. Using a dictionary, find two other meanings of the word *feature*.

A. **VOCABULARY** Here are some words from Reading 1. Read their definitions. Then complete each sentence.

> **attitude** (*noun*) 🔑 the way you think, feel, or behave
>
> **consequences** (*noun*) 🔑 things that follow as a result or effect of something else
>
> **consumer** (*noun*) 🔑 a person who buys things or uses services
>
> **disposable** (*adjective*) something you can throw away
>
> **factor** (*noun*) 🔑 one of the things that influences a decision or situation
>
> **feature** (*noun*) 🔑 an important or noticeable part of something
>
> **habit** (*noun*) 🔑 something that somebody does very often
>
> **persuade** (*verb*) 🔑 to cause somebody to do something by giving him or her good reason
>
> **possession** (*noun*) 🔑 something that you have or own

🔑 Oxford 3000™ words

1. Polluting the environment has serious _____ for our society. For example, scientists say that air pollution can result in many health problems.

2. Miguelina's favorite _____ is the gold necklace her grandmother gave her.

3. Eating junk food is a bad _____. It's very unhealthy!

4. There are fewer people shopping in the mall this year than there were last year. The average _____ is spending less than last year.

5. My brother worked hard to _____ me to recycle more of my trash. I thought it would be too much trouble, but I changed my mind.

6. My printer has a new _____ I really like. It can scan photos and print them.

7. Sandra has a very positive _____. She always has a cheerful outlook.

8. I can't decide which new car to buy, but the main _____ in my decision will be the price.

9. For the meal, we used _____ glasses and plates. We didn't want to wash dishes after the meal, so we threw them away.

iQ ONLINE **B.** Go online for more practice with the vocabulary.

C. PREVIEW This article discusses some of the reasons we have too much trash and suggests some possible solutions. In the article, the author uses the term *throwaway society*. What do you think *throwaway society* means?

☐ It's a society that recycles a lot.

☐ It's a society that throws away a lot.

☐ It's a society that isn't important.

D. QUICK WRITE Write your responses to the questions below before you read the article. Be sure to use this section for your Unit Assignment.

1. If something you own is broken, do you usually fix it or do you usually buy something new?

2. What problems do you see with all of the trash that people throw away each year?

WORK WITH THE READING

》 **A.** Read the article and gather information about saving what you have or buying new things.

Think Before You Toss

"Why don't you just take them to the shoe repairman? He'll put new soles[1] on, shine them up, and they'll be good for many more years," my grandfather suggested. I was complaining that my favorite shoes were falling apart after only six months.

"Grandpa, that shoe repairman went out of business years ago. No one repairs shoes anymore. And really, I don't mind. I'd rather buy a new pair of shoes, even if they don't last[2] that long."

"Nothing's built to last anymore," he sighed.

1　Perhaps Grandpa has a point[3]. In our modern world, when something wears out, we throw it away and buy a replacement. If a shirt is torn or a coffee machine breaks, you throw it away. The problem is that countries around the world have growing mountains of trash because people are throwing out more trash than ever before. For example, in the United States, the amount of trash per person more than doubled from 1960 to 2014.

2　How did we become a throwaway society? First of all, it is now easier to replace an item than to spend time and money to repair it. Thanks to modern manufacturing and technology, companies are able to produce items quickly and inexpensively. Products are plentiful and prices are low, so we would rather buy something new than repair it. Even if we did want to repair something, many items—from toasters to TVs—are almost impossible to repair. These products contain many tiny, complicated parts. Some even contain small computer chips. It's easier to throw these items away and buy new ones than to fix them.

3　Another contributing **factor** is our love of **disposable** products. As busy people, we are always looking for ways to save time and make our lives easier. Why should we use cloth kitchen towels? It is easier to use a paper towel once and toss it out. Companies manufacture thousands of different kinds of disposable items: paper plates, plastic cups, cameras, and razors for

---

[1] **soles:** the part of the shoe that covers the bottom
[2] **last:** to remain in good condition

[3] **have a point:** to have an important comment in a discussion

shaving, to name a few. Because these products aren't designed to last, companies know that **consumers** will have to replace them, buying them over and over again. "What's wrong with that?" you ask. The problem is that disposable products are contributing to our trash problem.

4   Our appetite for new products also contributes to the problem. We are addicted to[4] buying new things. As consumers, we want the latest clothes, the best TVs, and cell phones with the newest **features**. Companies tell us to buy, buy, and buy. Advertisements **persuade** us that newer is better and that we will be happier with the latest products. The result is that we throw away useful **possessions** to make room for new ones. In the U.S., when consumers get rid of electronics, 70 percent of them go to a dump. Only about 30 percent of electronics are recycled.

5   All around the world, we can see the **consequences** of this throwaway lifestyle. Dumpsites are mountains of garbage that just keep getting bigger. To decrease the amount of trash and to protect the environment, more governments are requiring people to recycle materials such as paper, plastic, and glass. However, only a small portion of what can be recycled is actually recycled. For example, in the United Kingdom, only 43 percent of household trash is actually

recycled. Even though recycling helps, it's not enough to solve our problem of too much trash.

6   Maybe there is another solution. First, we need to repair our possessions instead of throwing them away. As consumers, we should think about how to fix something to make it last. Furthermore, we need to rethink our **attitudes** about spending. Do we really need the latest clothing styles when our closets are full of clothes? Repairing our possessions and changing our spending **habits** may be the best way to reduce the amount of trash and take care of our environment.

What can you do to waste less?	
Think before you buy.	Sell it.
Fix it or get it repaired.	Give it away.
Recycle it.	

---

[4] **addicted to:** unable to stop

B. **Answer these questions. Underline the sentences in the reading where you found the answers.**

1. What is the grandfather's opinion about products made today?

    _____

2. Why are there "growing mountains of trash" in various parts of the world?

    _____

3. The author says that we are a "throwaway society." What does that mean?

    _____

4. What examples does the author give of disposable items?

   _____

5. Why do consumers like disposable products?

   _____

6. Why do companies like disposable products?

   _____

7. What is the result of our addiction to buying new things?

   _____

8. The author gives her opinion in the last paragraph. What is it?

   _____

C. Answer these questions.

1. What examples does the author give of products that we usually don't repair?

2. Why are companies able to make products more quickly and at lower cost?

3. Why are some things difficult to repair?

4. What are four reasons we throw things away?

5. Why do consumers often get rid of useful possessions?

6. What do these numbers refer to in the article?
   a. 1960–2012: _____
   b. 70 percent, 30 percent: _____
   c. 43 percent: _____

D. Look back at Reading 1 and find three questions. Write them below. Does the author already know the answers? Why does she ask them? Discuss your answer with a partner.

_____

_____

_____

E. Match the causes with the effects.

_____ 1. People are throwing more things away.

_____ 2. People think that new things are better.

_____ 3. Prices are low.

_____ 4. Products are not designed to last for a long time

_____ 5. Some products have complicated parts.

a. People need to replace disposable products.

b. People would rather buy a new item than repair an old item.

c. There are large quantities of trash around the world.

d. They are difficult to repair.

e. Useful possessions are thrown away.

iQ ONLINE **F.** Go online to read _Sell Your Stuff Online_ and check your comprehension.

WRITE WHAT YOU THINK

A. Discuss these questions in a group.

1. What items (clothing, electronics, sports equipment) have you recently thrown away? Could the items have been repaired? Why or why not? Did you replace them with something new?

2. Think of something that is still useful, but that you no longer want. What can you do with that item instead of throwing it away?

3. Do you think recycling is important? What kind of things do you recycle?

B. Choose one of the questions and write a multiple sentence response. Look back at your Quick Write on page 150 as you think about what you learned.

Question: _____

My Response: _____

_____

_____

_____

A **fact** is something that people generally agree is true. Facts are sometimes supported by statistics or other numbers.

> Water freezes at 0° Celsius.
> Paper is one of the easiest materials to recycle.
> In the United States, 18 percent of old TVs are recycled.

An **opinion** is what a person thinks about something. Another person may not agree.

> English is an easy language to learn.
> Consumers are more interested in a product's price than in its quality.
> Advertising has a bad influence on our spending habits.

When reading, it's helpful to understand the difference between facts and opinions. Some words that can indicate an opinion are: (*not*) *think*, (*not*) *believe*, (*not*) *feel*, and *in my opinion*.

> I **don't think** English is an easy language to learn.
> The author **believes** advertising has a bad influence on our spending habits.

A. Read these sentences from Reading 1. Write *F* (fact) or *O* (opinion). Then compare your answers with a partner.

_____ 1.   It is now easier to replace an item than to repair it.

_____ 2.   Many materials such as paper, plastic, and glass can be recycled, but only a small percentage of these are actually recycled.

_____ 3.   Perhaps recycling is not the answer.

_____ 4.   We should think about repairing something before we toss it in the trash.

_____ 5.   We are all responsible for taking care of our environment.

_____ 6.   People are throwing away twice as much trash as they did 40 years ago.

B. Write a sentence with an opinion and a fact about each topic. For your opinion sentences, use (*not*) *think*, (*not*) *believe*, (*not*) *feel*, or *in my opinion*.

1. color

    Fact: _Colors can affect how people feel._ _____

    Opinion: _I think pink is a beautiful color._ _____

2. cell phones

Fact: _____

Opinion: _____

3. recycling plastic, paper, and glass

Fact: _____

Opinion: _____

4. shopping online

Fact: _____

Opinion: _____

 C. Go online for more practice with identifying fact and opinion.

READING 2 | In Praise of the Throwaway Society

 You are going to read a blog post. In the blog, a man gives his opinion about the throwaway society. Use the blog post to gather information and ideas for your Unit Assignment.

PREVIEW THE READING

A. **VOCABULARY** Here are some words from Reading 2. Read the sentences. Then match each underlined word with its definition on page 157.

1. I've never heard the term *throwaway society*. What does it mean?

2. Sun Joon is a very materialistic person. She seems more interested in shopping than making friends.

3. Paul's old jacket is patched on the elbows where it used to be ripped.

4. If there's a significant amount of snow, the schools will close.

5. Do you think that life forms exist in outer space?

6. New flowers in the garden are a sign that spring is here.

7. My old cell phone works pretty well, but I really want to get a new model.

8. After the soccer game, Khalid put on a fresh shirt and put his dirty one in the wash.

9. Kevin and Tanya made a <u>budget</u> for March, but they spent more than they had planned.

10. Yuki thought that the new phone would cost $50, but the <u>actual</u> cost was higher.

a. _____ (*noun*) a plan of how much money you will have and how you will spend it

b. _____ (*verb*) to be real; to live

c. _____ (*adjective*) clean or new

d. _____ (*adjective*) believing that money and possessions are the most important things in life

e. _____ (*noun*) a certain style of an item that a company makes

f. _____ (*adjective*) covered with cloth to repair a hole

g. _____ (*noun*) something that shows that something exists, is happening, or may happen in the future

h. _____ (*adjective*) important or large enough to be noticed

i. _____ (*noun*) a word or group of words

j. _____ (*adjective*) that really happened; real

iQ ONLINE   **B.** Go online for more practice with the vocabulary.

Tip for Success

Remember that when writing online, people often use informal language. For example, they may use informal words and phrases. (stuff = things) They may also begin sentences with *But* or *And*.

C. PREVIEW The author of the blog has an opinion that is different from the opinion given in Reading 1. What do you think he will say about a throwaway society?

☐ In a throwaway society, no one should recycle.

☐ A throwaway society shows that people are doing well.

☐ Wealthy people don't need to throw anything away.

D. QUICK WRITE Some people feel that it is foolish to repair old things. They believe that we should just buy new things. What are some advantages of buying new things? Write a few sentences. Be sure to use this section for your Unit Assignment.

WORK WITH THE READING

🔊 **A.** Read the blog post and gather information about saving what you have or buying new things.

Mad Anthony

Opinions and thoughts on politics, technology, life, and other stuff

Home   Log in

In Praise of the Throwaway Society

JANUARY 26, 2015   COMMENTS 16

About

Links

Archives

January
February
March
April
May
June
July
August
September
October
November
December

1   Yesterday, I heard someone use the phrase *throwaway society*, which got me thinking. Usually, the **term** *throwaway society* is used as a way of saying that we are too **materialistic**. It means that too much of our stuff today is of poor quality instead of being built to last.

2   I see things the opposite way. The fact that we live in a throwaway society isn't a **sign** that things are worse than they used to be. It is a sign that things are better than they have ever been. True, we don't repair things as much as we used to. But that's because we don't have to and don't want to, not because we can't. And it's better that way.

3   I say this because being able to replace instead of repair shows that people are wealthy. What would you rather have: an old repaired laptop or the latest **model**? A pair of socks with the hole **patched** or a **fresh** pair? Some people think that products today are less dependable than they used to be. But most people would rather have something with a newer design, and they vote with their wallets[1].

4   I think there are three reasons for this. First, lower prices. Today, because of technology, it costs less to make items, so they sell for less. When the price difference is small or when it costs more to fix an item than to replace it, consumers naturally decide to pick up a new one. Second, increased wealth. People have more money than they did in the past, and because of lower prices, they can afford more things. A hundred years ago, most people had one or two sets of clothes. Those clothes were valuable and expensive and formed a **significant** part of their **budget**. Now, you can get a nice sweater for a few dollars. It isn't expensive at all. When that sweater gets a hole in it, you toss it and buy a new one because you can afford to.

5   Third, increased features. Thanks to advances in technology, products are getting better all the time, especially electronics. There is a good chance that the latest model includes some cool features that didn't **exist** when your old one

[1] **vote with their wallets:** show their opinion by buying what they want

was made. Now, you can get a high-definition[2] digital camera that is small enough to fit in your hand. You can get cell phones that have everything from email to video to GPS[3]. In fact, I hardly ever use my phone for an **actual** phone call anymore because it can do so many other wonderful things. You see, the benefit of increased features is another reason to buy something new. So throw something out today! The throwaway society shows us how good things are.

[2] **high definition:** very good quality
[3] **GPS (global positioning system):** digital tool that can tell you your location

[4] **fooling around:** not taking something seriously; playing or experimenting with something

B. Read the statements. Are they true or false according to the author of Reading 2? Write *T* (true) and *F* (false).

____ 1. Most people think that *throwaway society* means we are too materialistic.

____ 2. The author thinks it is too bad that we don't repair things as much as we used to.

____ 3. People vote with their wallets by not buying new things.

____ 4. Because of technology, the cost of new items has gone up.

____ 5. Today more people can easily afford to buy new clothes.

____ 6. New products have too many features to be useful.

____ 7. Our throwaway society is going to cause problems in the future.

C. Circle the answer that best completes each statement. Then underline the place in the reading where you found the answer.

1. According to Mad Anthony, the throwaway society is a sign that …
   a. society has become too materialistic.
   b. things are worse than they used to be.
   c. things are better than they have ever been.

2. Mad Anthony says that …
   a. people would rather have something new.
   b. we can't repair things as easily as before.
   c. replacing instead of repairing is a sign of a weak society.

3. People buy clothing instead of repairing it because …
   a. clothing today is very valuable.
   b. it doesn't cost much to buy new clothes.
   c. clothing forms a significant part of their budget.

4. The author thinks that one reason people buy new things is …
   a. their old model doesn't have the latest features.
   b. cell phones are no longer useful for making actual phone calls.
   c. too many features make new models complicated.

5. The author of this reading thinks that people should …
   a. fix items rather than replace things.
   b. take pictures with their cell phones.
   c. throw things away when they're old.

D. Complete each sentence with information from Reading 2. Then look at
Reading 2 to check your answers.

1. Today, because of technology, it costs _____ to make items,

   so products sell for _____.

2. When the price difference is _____ or when it costs

   _____ to fix an item than to _____ it,

   consumers naturally decide to pick up a new one.

3. People have _____ money than they did in the past, and

   because of _____ prices, people can _____

   more things.

4. Thanks to advances in technology, products are getting

   _____ all the time.

5. The _____ of increased features is another

   _____ to buy something new.

WRITE WHAT YOU THINK

A. Discuss these questions in a group. Look back at your Quick Write on
page 157 as you think about what you learned.

1. Do you think it is better to save and wear old clothing or to buy new,
trendy clothes? Why?

2. Mad Anthony gives reasons to support his opinion that the throwaway society is a good thing. Do you think these are good reasons? Why or why not?

B. Go online to watch the video about a man who recycles items found in the trash. Then check your comprehension.

VIDEO VOCABULARY

dumpster *(n.)* large outdoor container for trash

gather up *(phr. v.)* to collect; pick up

notion *(n.)* idea

refuse *(n.)* trash or things thrown away

Critical Thinking **Tip**

Question 2 asks you to **devise**, or think of, a new way to use an unwanted item. **Devising** means that you have to put information and ideas together in a new way.

C. Think about the unit video, Reading 1, and Reading 2 as you discuss these questions. Then choose one question and write a response.

1. What are some of the advantages of buying new things instead of fixing old things? Give examples.

2. Some people make new things from old items. For example, some artists make jewelry from old computer parts. What are some new ways you can use something you normally throw away?

Vocabulary Skill   Phrasal verbs

A **phrasal verb** is a *verb* + a *particle*. Some examples of particles are *in, out, up, over, by, down,* and *away.* When a particle is added to a verb, it often creates a new meaning.

> I want to **watch** the game on TV tonight.   (watch = look at)
> **Watch out** for ice on the stairs!   (watch out = be careful)

Many phrasal verbs have more than one meaning.

> He **picked up** the book and started to read.   (lifted)
> Abdullah **picked up** his friend in his new red car.   (gave a ride to)
> The wind **picked up** in the afternoon.   (increased)

Some phrasal verbs are **separable**. They can be separated by objects.

> He **picked up** the book.   Yolanda **threw away** her old shoes.
> He **picked** the book **up**.   Yolanda **threw** her old shoes **away**.

Some phrasal verbs are **inseparable**. They cannot be separated by an object.

> ✓ Ollie **fell down** the stairs.   ✓ Eva **stopped by** my house yesterday.
> ✗ Ollie **fell** the stairs **down**.   ✗ Eva **stopped** my house **by** yesterday.

A. Read the sentences. Then circle the answer that best matches the meaning of each bold phrasal verb.

1. I **wore out** my favorite jeans, so I bought a new pair.
   a. repaired   b. used too much

2. Don't **throw out** the newspaper. I want to read the sports page.
   a. put in the trash   b. put outside

3. It's raining, so I'm going to **put on** my raincoat.
   a. wash   b. wear

4. You shouldn't **throw away** plastic bottles. You should recycle them.
   a. reuse   b. put in the trash

5. The shoes at that store are very cheap, but they are not good quality, so they **fall apart** easily.
   a. look nice   b. break into pieces

B. Rewrite the sentences putting the object between the verb and the particle.

1. We picked up the children from school.

   We picked the children up from school.

2. Please throw away your trash. Don't leave it in the park.

   _____

3. Put on your hat. It's very cold outside!

   _____

4. I'm going to throw out my old watch and buy a new one.

   _____

5. I walk a lot, so I wear out my shoes quickly.

   _____

iQ ONLINE   **C.** Go online for more practice with phrasal verbs.

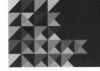

WRITING

At the end of this unit, you will write an opinion paragraph. This paragraph will include specific information from the readings and your own ideas.

Writing Skill | Using sentence variety

When you write, it's important to use different types of sentences. Using different types of sentences makes your writing more interesting to read. Here are some ways to improve your **sentence variety**.

- Use long and short sentences.
- If you have too many short sentences, combine two sentences into one with a coordinating conjunction (*and*, *but*, or *so*).
- Use questions and imperatives.

Look at these examples from Reading 1.

> Perhaps Grandpa has a point. In our modern world, when something wears out, we throw it away and buy a replacement.

> Products are plentiful and prices are low, so we would rather buy something new than repair it.

> Why should we use cloth kitchen towels? It is easier to use a paper towel once and toss it out.

A. WRITING MODEL Read the model paragraph. Then do tasks 1–4 below. Compare your answers with a partner.

Do you prefer to fix what you have or buy new things? I usually fix the things I have, but I always buy new shoes. I love buying shoes. I already have lots of shoes in different styles and colors, but I always find a new pair that I want to buy. Sometimes after class, I meet my friend Sue. We have coffee, and then we go shopping for shoes at the new shopping center downtown. It's a nice way to spend the afternoon. Are your shoes old and worn out? Don't fix them. Buy a new pair. It's fun!

1. Circle the short sentences in the paragraph.

2. Underline the long sentences in the paragraph.

3. Put a check (✓) next to the questions.

4. Put a star next to the imperatives.

B. Take the two short sentences and make them one long sentence. Use *and*, *but*, or *so*.

1. I try to recycle things. Other people in my family usually just throw things away.

   _____

2. It was raining all day. My clothes got wet.

   _____

3. I wasn't wearing a raincoat. I might catch a cold.

   _____

4. Vladimir likes to buy new clothes. His sister Maria likes to buy new clothes, too.

   _____

5. I wish vacation were longer. School starts on Monday.

   _____

C. WRITING MODEL Rewrite the model paragraph below and use more sentence variety. You can combine sentences, change sentences, and add more sentences to the paragraph.

Earlier this year, some students noticed that recycling was difficult at our school. There were no containers to collect paper for recycling. People just threw paper away. Also, many students drink bottled water. They throw bottles in the trash without thinking. Student organizers made posters about recycling. They put containers for recycling paper in every classroom and office. In one month, there was a significant increase in the amount of paper in the containers. There were also more bottles in the containers. The organizers are very happy with the results. They hope people's habits continue to change. They hope attitudes change, too.

D. Write an outline for a paragraph giving your opinion on this statement: *Everyone should be required to recycle.* Write some notes to help you state your opinion in a topic sentence, give reasons to support your opinion, and form a concluding sentence.

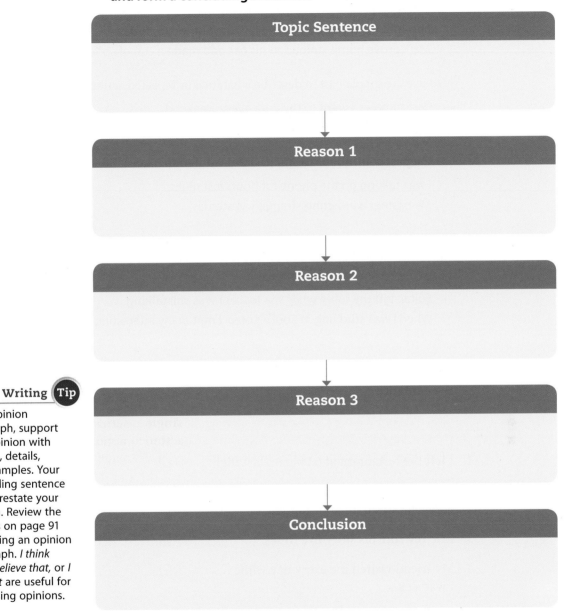

Topic Sentence

Reason 1

Reason 2

Reason 3

Conclusion

Writing Tip

In an opinion paragraph, support your opinion with reasons, details, and examples. Your concluding sentence should restate your opinion. Review the phrases on page 91 for writing an opinion paragraph. *I think that, I believe that,* or *I feel that* are useful for expressing opinions.

E. Write a paragraph based on your notes from Activity D. Use complete sentences with a variety of sentence types. Include some useful expressions for writing an opinion paragraph.

F. Share your writing with a classmate. Did you use useful sentences for giving opinions? Did you use a variety of sentence types? Rewrite your paragraph based on the feedback from your classmate.

iQ ONLINE **G.** Go online for more practice with sentence variety.

Grammar | Simple past and past continuous

Use the **simple past** to describe a single completed action or a series of completed actions in the past:

> I **bought** the new novel by my favorite author yesterday.
> Mark **drove** home, **unloaded** his car, and **made** a cup of coffee.

Also use the simple past to describe a habitual or repeated action in the past.

> Last summer, I **went** to the park every weekend.
> I **sent** Leila three emails, but she never replied.

Use the **past continuous** to emphasize the duration of an action in the past.

> I **was talking** on the phone for hours last night.
> My brother **was acting** strangely yesterday.

If a past event was interrupted by another event or series of events, use *while* or *when* with the past continuous for the interrupted event. Use the simple past for the event or events that interrupted it.

> Sultan **left** the room <u>while</u> the teacher **was** still **talking**.
> <u>When</u> I **was studying** in South Korea, I **met** many interesting people.

A. Read the sentences. Check (✓) the function of the simple past (in bold) in the sentence.

	single action	series of actions	repeated action
1. I **left** the restaurant at 6:00 p.m. last night.	☐	☐	☐
2. When the president **came** into the room, everyone **stood** up and **clapped**.	☐	☐	☐
3. Eric **rewrote** his story five times.	☐	☐	☐
4. My friend **visited** me every day while I was sick.	☐	☐	☐
5. Someone **stole** my bike last week.	☐	☐	☐
6. Jessica **finished** her letter, **put** it in an envelope, and **took** it to the post office.	☐	☐	☐

B. Read the sentences. Check (✓) the function of the past continuous (in bold) in the sentence.

	duration	interrupted action
1. Jim broke his leg while he **was playing** soccer.	☐	☐
2. I **was watching** TV all weekend.	☐	☐
3. When Natalia **was working** in the science lab, she discovered a mistake.	☐	☐
4. You **were complaining** the whole time at the restaurant last night.	☐	☐

iQ ONLINE **C.** Go online for more practice with the simple past and the past continuous.

D. Go online for the grammar expansion.

Unit Assignment Write an opinion paragraph

UNIT OBJECTIVE ▶▶▶▶ In this assignment, you will write an opinion paragraph. As you prepare your paragraph, think about the Unit Question, "Is it better to save what you have or buy new things?" Use information from Reading 1, Reading 2, the unit video, and your work in this unit to support your opinion. Refer to the Self-Assessment checklist on page 168.

iQ ONLINE Go to the Online Writing Tutor for a writing model and alternate Unit Assignments.

PLAN AND WRITE

A. BRAINSTORM Brainstorm ideas about the Unit Question. Write as many ideas as you can.

Tip for Success

In a test situation, you need to quickly organize your ideas before you write your answer. An informal outline is a quick and easy way to plan your writing.

B. PLAN Make an informal outline to organize your ideas.

It's better to _____

Reason 1: _____

Reason 2: _____

Reason 3: _____

C. **WRITE** Use your **PLAN** notes to write your paragraph. Go to *iQ Online* to use the Online Writing Tutor.

1. Write your paragraph, using your notes from Activity B. Start with a clear topic sentence and include ideas that support your opinion. Finish with a strong concluding sentence. Try to use some useful expressions for giving opinions, some phrasal verbs, and the simple past or past continuous.

2. Look at the Self-Assessment checklist to guide your writing.

REVISE AND EDIT

A. **PEER REVIEW** Read your partner's paragraph. Then go online and use the Peer Review worksheet. Discuss the review with your partner.

B. **REWRITE** Based on your partner's review, revise and rewrite your paragraph.

C. **EDIT** Complete the Self-Assessment checklist as you prepare to write the final draft of your paragraph. Be prepared to hand in your work or discuss it in class.

Yes	No	SELF-ASSESSMENT
☐	☐	Do you give a strong opinion and support it with facts?
☐	☐	Do you use a variety of sentence types to make your writing more interesting to read?
☐	☐	Do you use simple past and past continuous verbs correctly?
☐	☐	Circle any phrasal verbs you used in your paragraph. Do they express your ideas clearly?
☐	☐	Does the paragraph include vocabulary from the unit?
☐	☐	Did you check the paragraph for punctuation, spelling, and grammar?

D. **REFLECT** Go to the Online Discussion Board to discuss these questions.

1. What is something new you learned in this unit?

2. Look back at the Unit Question—Is it better to save what you have or buy new things? Is your answer different now than when you started the unit? If yes, how is it different? Why?

TRACK YOUR SUCCESS

Circle the words and phrases you have learned in this unit.

Nouns	Verbs	Adjectives
attitude 🔑 AWL	exist 🔑	actual 🔑
budget 🔑	persuade 🔑	disposable AWL
consequence 🔑 AWL	**Phrasal Verbs**	fresh 🔑
consumer 🔑 AWL	fall apart	materialistic
factor 🔑 AWL	fall down	patched
feature 🔑 AWL	pick up	significant 🔑 AWL
habit 🔑	put on	
model 🔑	stop by	
possession 🔑	throw away	
sign 🔑	throw out	
term 🔑	watch out	
	wear out	

🔑 Oxford 3000™ words
AWL Academic Word List

Check (✓) the skills you learned. If you need more work on a skill, refer to the page(s) in parentheses.

READING ☐	I can identify facts and opinions. (p. 155)
VOCABULARY ☐	I can use phrasal verbs. (p. 161)
WRITING ☐	I can use sentence variety. (p. 163)
GRAMMAR ☐	I can use the simple past and the past continuous. (p. 166)
UNIT OBJECTIVE ▶▶▶▶ ☐	I can gather information and ideas to write an opinion paragraph.

READING ▶ synthesizing information
VOCABULARY ▶ collocations
WRITING ▶ writing an explanatory paragraph
GRAMMAR ▶ adverbs of manner and degree

UNIT QUESTION

How can we prevent diseases?

A Discuss these questions with your classmates.

1. When was the last time you were sick? How did you feel?
   How did you get sick?

2. What are some things you do to avoid getting sick?

3. Look at the photo. Who do you think the people are?
   What are they doing?

B Listen to *The Q Classroom* online. Then answer these questions.

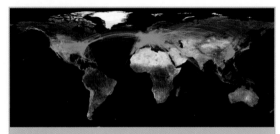

Disease can spread anywhere in 24 hours.

1. What six ways to prevent disease did the speakers mention? Fill in the chart below. Then for each one, check (✓) how often you do it. When you finish, discuss your chart with your classmates.

Ways to prevent diseases		Always	Sometimes	Rarely	Never
a.	eat right				
b.					
c.					
d.					
e.					
f.					

2. Do you agree with Sophy and Felix that people should wear face masks or stay home when they are sick? Why or why not?

iQ ONLINE **C** Go to the Online Discussion Board to discuss the Unit Question with your classmates.

D Work with a partner. Match the name of each illness with the correct photo.

| diabetes | malaria | influenza (flu) |
| asthma | skin cancer | tuberculosis (TB) |

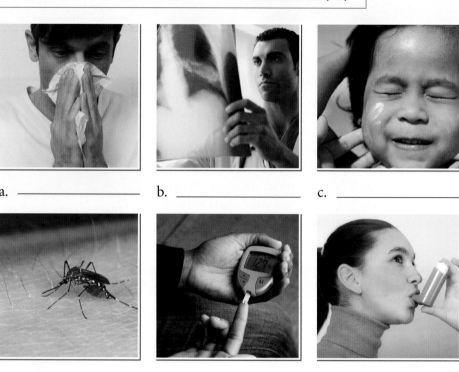

a. _____   b. _____   c. _____

d. _____   e. _____   f. _____

E Write the illness from Activity D next to the correct description.

1. _____: Sun exposure is the leading cause of this disease. This disease causes cells to grow quickly.

2. _____: This is a serious disease that you can get from mosquito bites.

3. _____: This disease affects the lungs and spreads from person to person very easily.

4. _____: This condition causes difficulty in breathing. Using an inhaler (something to help people breathe more easily) can help.

5. _____: With this disease, the body cannot process sugar correctly.

6. _____: With this common illness, a person is sick for one to two weeks.

F Work with a partner. Discuss illnesses that spread from person to person.

READING 1 | Flu FAQ (Frequently Asked Questions)

UNIT OBJECTIVE ▶▶▶▶ You are going to read a Web page from a health website. Use the Web page to gather information and ideas for your Unit Assignment.

PREVIEW THE READING

A. **VOCABULARY** Here are some words from Reading 1. Read the sentences. Then write each <u>underlined</u> word next to the correct definition.

1. Yesterday <u>approximately</u> 50 students were home with the flu. I don't know the exact number.

2. You should <u>cover</u> your baby with extra blankets in the winter so he doesn't get cold.

3. I hope my cold doesn't <u>develop</u> into a bad cough. It's already worse than it was yesterday.

4. During the <u>epidemic</u>, every home in the town had at least one sick family member.

5. Colds are <u>extremely</u> common among school children during winter. Both of my children have colds right now.

6. If you have a cold and you sneeze on other people, you can <u>infect</u> them.

7. Your overall health is directly <u>related to</u> how well you eat and how often you exercise.

8. Pria had a <u>severe</u> pain in her back, so I took her to the hospital.

9. A sore throat is a common <u>symptom</u> of a cold.

10. A <u>virus</u> causes the common cold. It spreads from person to person quickly.

a. _____ (*adjective*) connected with something

b. _____ (*noun*) something that shows that you have an illness

c. _____ (*noun*) a living thing that is too small to see but that makes you sick

d. _____ (*verb*) to put something on or in front of something else to protect it

e. _____ (*verb*) to give a disease to someone

f. _____ (*adjective*) very bad

g. _____ (*adverb*) very

h. _____ (*verb*) to grow slowly, increase, or change into something else

i. _____ (*adverb*) about; not exactly

j. _____ (*noun*) a disease that many people in a place have at the same time

 B. Go online for more practice with the vocabulary.

C. **PREVIEW** This online FAQ (Frequently Asked Questions) page is from a health website about the flu. FAQ pages state commonly asked questions about a topic, followed by the answers. Read the questions in the headings. Which ones can you answer without reading the answers?

D. **QUICK WRITE** Think about the last time you had a bad cold or the flu. Write your responses to the questions before you read the Web page. Be sure to use this section for your Unit Assignment.

1. What were your symptoms?

2. How long were you sick? Did you stay home from school or work?

3. What helped you feel better while you were sick?

WORK WITH THE READING

A. Read the Web page and gather information about how we can prevent diseases.

Flu FAQ (Frequently Asked Questions)

Flu season is coming! Are you prepared? Here are answers to your questions!

What is the flu?

1   The flu, short for *influenza*, is a **virus** that passes easily from person to person. Every year, millions of people miss work and school because of the seasonal flu. Seasonal flu exists worldwide. Usually the flu season is in the winter months, but in warm climates, the flu occurs during the rainy season.

What are the symptoms of the flu?

2   Flu **symptoms** include fever, cough, sore throat, body aches, headache, chills, and fatigue[1]. These symptoms usually show up quickly, **developing** within three to six hours of exposure to the virus. With the flu,

[1] **fatigue:** great tiredness

you may start the day feeling fine, only to end up feeling terrible a few hours later.

What's the difference between the flu and a cold?

3   Both are respiratory[2] illnesses, but they are caused by different viruses. Although the symptoms can be similar, flu symptoms are more **severe** and include a high fever and body aches. Cold symptoms include a runny or stuffy[3] nose and a cough. You may have a slight fever with a cold, but in general, cold symptoms are milder and only last about seven days. The flu can last up to two weeks. It is much more likely to develop into a serious illness and require hospitalization.

Who gets the flu?

4   The seasonal flu is very common all over the world. In the United States, 5 to 20 percent of the population gets the flu every year. After you have had the flu, you have immunity[4] to that virus. You will not get that particular virus again. However, new flu viruses appear every year. Even if you have the flu this year, you will not have immunity to next year's virus. Some people get the flu every year.

Why is the flu dangerous?

5   The flu is especially dangerous for children aged 2 and under, adults over 65 years old, and people in poor health. These people may not be able to fight the virus and can become **extremely** sick. Every year in the U.S., there are **approximately** 36,000 deaths **related to** the seasonal flu.

How does the flu spread?

6   Coughing or sneezing spreads flu viruses from person to person. A virus can live in a tiny drop of liquid from a cough for several hours, and it can live on a surface such as a table for up to 24 hours. A person can **infect** others before flu symptoms even develop and up to five days after becoming sick. You can pass the flu to someone else before you know you are sick.

What's a flu epidemic?

7   A flu **epidemic** is when many people have the flu at the same time, and the number of infected people increases rapidly. Worldwide, annual flu epidemics result in about 3 to 5 million cases of severe illness, and about 250,000 to 500,000 deaths.

How can I avoid getting the flu?

8   Many people get a flu vaccine[5] before the flu season starts. The U.S. Center for Disease Control and Prevention says that flu vaccines can prevent 70 percent to 90 percent of infections in healthy people under age 65. However, each year there are new, unknown viruses. Therefore, scientists must develop new vaccines each year. It can take 6 months to a year to develop these vaccines. For some viruses, there is no vaccine.

What else can I do?

9   There are many things you can do to stay healthy and prevent the spread of the flu.

- Wash your hands often with soap and water or a liquid hand cleaner. Hand washing is the best way to prevent the spread of flu viruses.
- **Cover** your nose and mouth with a tissue when you cough or sneeze. Throw the tissue in the trash after you use it. If you don't have a tissue, cover your mouth with your arm or shirtsleeve instead of your hands.
- Avoid touching your eyes, nose, or mouth. Viruses can spread this way.
- Avoid sick people.

---

[2] **respiratory**: related to breathing
[3] **stuffy**: blocked, making it difficult to breathe
[4] **immunity**: the ability to not get a disease
[5] **vaccine**: a medicine given to people to protect them from a particular disease

B. Circle the answer to each question.

1. What is the purpose of this Web page?
    a. To provide detailed information about flu deaths around the world.
    b. To tell readers how to stay healthy and why they should get a vaccine.
    c. To provide basic information about the flu and how to prevent it.
    d. To scare readers so that they get the flu vaccine every year.

2. Why do people often think a cold is the flu?
    a. Flu symptoms are more severe than cold symptoms.
    b. Cold and flu symptoms can be similar.
    c. A cold only lasts about a week.
    d. Viruses cause colds and the flu.

3. Why is it important to avoid people who are sick with the flu?
    a. They could infect you with the flu.
    b. They should stay in bed.
    c. You may spread a cold to them and make them sicker.
    d. They might not have washed their hands.

4. Based on the information from the FAQs, which of the following can you infer?
    a. Governments give free flu vaccines.
    b. People don't know what the flu is.
    c. The flu is the most difficult global health problem today.
    d. Understanding the flu is important for people around the world.

C. Compare a cold and the flu using the Venn diagram below. Write facts about the flu inside the circle on the left. Write facts about a cold inside the circle on the right. Write facts that are true about both a cold and the flu in the middle.

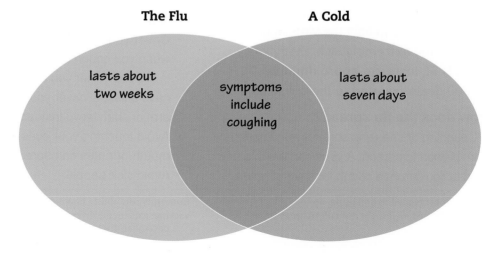

The Flu   A Cold

lasts about two weeks

symptoms include coughing

lasts about seven days

D. Find the answers to the questions in Reading 1.

1. What percentage of people in the United States gets the flu every year?

    _____

2. Why is the flu especially dangerous for elderly people?

    _____

3. After you are infected with the flu, how long will it be before you have symptoms?

    _____

4. How many deaths are related to the flu worldwide each year?

    _____

5. What percentage of healthy people under the age of 65 can flu vaccines help in the U.S. every year?

    _____

6. How can you prevent the flu from spreading?

    _____

E. Look back at the reading on pages 174–175 and answer these questions. Then discuss your answers in a group.

1. What is an additional question to add to the FAQ page? Why would this be a good question to add?

    _____

    _____

2. What do you think the answer might be?

    _____

    _____

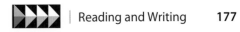 **F. Go online to read *The Common Cold* and check your comprehension.**

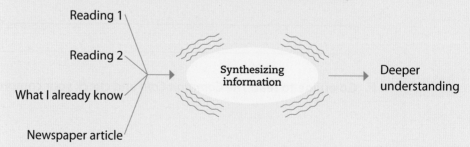

WRITE WHAT YOU THINK

A. Discuss these questions in a group.

1. The reading gives tips on how to avoid getting a cold or the flu. What are some other things you can do?

2. Some people worry a lot about catching the flu from others, and some people are not very concerned. How concerned are you, on a scale from 1 to 10 (10 = extremely concerned, 1 = not concerned at all)? Explain your answers.

3. What other illnesses or diseases are you interested in learning more about? What do you want to know about them?

B. Choose one of the questions and write a response. Look back at your Quick Write on page 174 as you think about what you learned.

Question: _____

My Response: _____

_____

_____

Reading Skill | **Synthesizing information**

When you **synthesize** information, you develop a new understanding about a topic by using information from more than one source. For example, you can synthesize information from two different readings to answer a question. You can also synthesize what you already know about a topic and the new information you are learning about that topic from an article you are reading.

Reading 1
Reading 2
What I already know
Newspaper article
→ Synthesizing information → Deeper understanding

Synthesizing information helps you deepen and expand your knowledge. It is also important because some test questions and writing assignments ask you to synthesize information you have read.

A. Answer these questions.

1. Think back to Reading 1. What information in the reading was new to you? What information did you already know?

    _____

    _____

2. Read these questions about Reading 1. Which one is a **synthesis** question? Which is a **main idea** question? Which is a **detail** question? Label each one.

    a. _____ How does the flu spread?

    b. _____ After reading this Web page, will you change any of your health habits? Why or why not?

    c. _____ How many people worldwide have a severe case of the flu every year?

3. Answer the questions in item 2. For the synthesis question, be sure to use information that you already know and information from the reading.

    a. _____

    b. _____

    c. _____

B. Read this paragraph. Then answer the synthesis questions, using what you already know, information in the paragraph, and the information in Reading 1.

> Just like humans, animals get flu viruses, too. These animal viruses rarely spread to humans, but occasionally they do. For example, an avian flu, also called bird flu, can spread from birds to humans. Once a person gets a virus from an animal, it then spreads very quickly from person to person, just like other types of the flu. Flu viruses that come from animals can be dangerous to humans and can make people extremely sick. People do not have immunity to these new viruses, and it can take a very long time for vaccines to be developed. There is often an increased possibility of death with illnesses like avian flu.

1. Is the avian flu more dangerous than the seasonal flu? Explain your answer.

    _____

    _____

2. How do you think that avian flu can spread from an animal to a human? How does it spread to many people?

_____

_____

 C. Go online for more practice with synthesizing information.

READING 2 | Watching Over the Health of Millions

 You are going to read a magazine article about doctors' efforts to prevent the spread of disease at large events. Use the article to gather information and ideas for your Unit Assignment.

PREVIEW THE READING

Vocabulary Skill Review

In Unit 7, you learned about phrasal verbs. Find the two phrasal verbs in paragraph 2 of Reading 1: *show up* and *end up*. Using a dictionary, find out if these phrasal verbs are separable or inseparable.

A. **VOCABULARY** Here are some words from Reading 2. Read their definitions. Then complete each sentence.

cooperation (*noun*) 🔑 working with other people to achieve a goal

decade (*noun*) 🔑 a period of ten years

mass (*adjective*) 🔑 involving a large number of people

outbreak (*noun*) the sudden start of something bad, such as a disease

quarantine (*verb*) to keep people who may have a disease away from other people in order to prevent the disease from spreading

risk (*noun*) 🔑 the possibility of something bad happening in the future

strategy (*noun*) 🔑 a plan that you use to achieve something

take steps (*phrasal verb*) to do a series of actions (to achieve something)

track (*verb*) 🔑 to find somebody/something by following the signs or information that they have left behind

vaccination (*noun*) the injection of a special medicine to protect people from getting a disease

🔑 Oxford 3000™ words

1. All of the students were required to get a _____ against tuberculosis, a serious disease.

2. Health officials held a _____ meeting of thousands of doctors to discuss the problem.

3. Many sick people arrived on the plane. The health officials decided to _____ all of them in a hospital to keep the disease from spreading.

4. Smoking cigarettes will increase your _____ of getting lung cancer.

5. The scientists tried to _____ the disease back to its original source.

6. Health is not just a local issue. It is a global issue and requires international _____.

7. It has taken us over a _____ of hard work to stop the disease from spreading.

8. In the elementary school, there was an _____ of the flu. About 30 percent of the kids got sick.

9. Researchers are trying to develop a good _____ to keep people healthy in large groups.

10. The doctors knew that they had to _____ immediately to prevent the disease from spreading.

iQ ONLINE **B.** Go online for more practice with the vocabulary.

C. PREVIEW You are going to read a magazine article about health problems that occur when there are large groups of people together. At such events, doctors work to prevent diseases from spreading. What do you think that doctors do to try to stop diseases from spreading?

☐ share knowledge   ☐ wash their hands
☐ use technology   ☐ cooperate with others

D. QUICK WRITE Diseases can spread quickly in public areas. What do you do to keep health problems from spreading? Think about what you do when you are at school, in a shopping mall, or on an airplane. Write a paragraph about the topic. Be sure to use this section for your Unit Assignment.

WORK WITH THE READING

》 **A. Read the magazine article and gather information about how we can prevent diseases.**

Watching Over the Health of Millions

1 Imagine you are a doctor specializing in infectious disease. Question: What is your worst nightmare[1]? Answer: A huge gathering of people from all over the world, with many sick or elderly people. Why? Because in this very crowded situation, diseases can spread rapidly and uncontrollably.

2 **Mass** gatherings, events with huge crowds of people, happen every year around the world, from the Hajj in Saudi Arabia to the World Cup. Global health experts realize that these mass gatherings can present serious health **risks** and can increase the spread of epidemics. Now doctors from many countries are sharing their knowledge about these health issues and are working together to find solutions.

3 In a recent report, experts from the Saudi Arabian Ministry of Health shared their knowledge about how to prevent the **outbreak** of global diseases at mass gatherings. The Ministry has **decades** of experience in managing the health of pilgrims[2] in the yearly Hajj to Mecca in Saudi Arabia. With more than two million pilgrims each year, the Hajj is the largest international mass gathering in the world. Many of the pilgrims arrive from low-income countries and have had little health care. Elderly or sick pilgrims want to complete this very important religious pilgrimage before they die, so they travel to Mecca with thousands of others.

4 According to the report, one of the first **strategies** is to make sure that all pilgrims receive a health screening[3]. Saudi health experts have designed special programs to screen pilgrims quickly and efficiently. For example, there is a separate terminal at the Jeddah International Airport for pilgrims. When pilgrims arrive by plane, they receive a health screening and **vaccinations**, if needed. There is a medical clinic at the airport for sick pilgrims. For pilgrims traveling within Saudi Arabia, officials check vaccination records and make sure people are up to date on all required vaccines.

5 Another important Saudi strategy is to use technology to **track** the outbreak of diseases. With many new technologies, experts are able to immediately report a person with a disease. That information quickly goes to all health officials, and organizers can **take steps** to control the outbreak. During a mass gathering, instant reporting is extremely important. During the 2009 Hajj, there was a global outbreak of the H1N1 bird flu pandemic[4]. Hajj organizers used technology to track and report cases of the flu. They used a cell phone system to collect information and the Internet to send reports instantly. Organizers also worked with the World Health Organization (WHO) to use rapid testing and to **quarantine** infected pilgrims. They were able to control the outbreak and prevent the spread to thousands of pilgrims.

6 The field of health for mass gatherings is growing. This is a very new field of medicine, and international **cooperation** is a key ingredient. The Saudi Ministry of Health has recently created a new diploma course in Mass Gathering and Disaster Medicine, based in Jeddah. The goal is to develop an international center for sharing knowledge. Zaid Memish from the Ministry of Health said that "multinational approaches to public health challenges are likely to become major factors in global health diplomacy and bringing the West a little closer to the East." International cooperation will help limit the spread of disease and lead to better health around the world.

---

[1] **nightmare:** a dream that is frightening
[2] **pilgrims:** people who travel to a holy place for religious reasons

[3] **health screening:** the testing or examining of a person for disease
[4] **pandemic:** outbreak of a disease that occurs in many areas of the world at one time

B. Answer these questions.

1. Why are large gatherings of people a doctor's nightmare?

   _____

2. What are some examples of mass gatherings?

   _____

3. What is the largest international mass gathering in the world?

   _____

4. What is the first strategy to keep pilgrims healthy?

   _____

5. Why is it important to quarantine people who are infected?

   _____

6. What is the second strategy that Saudis use?

   _____

C. Read the statements. Write *T* (true) or *F* (false). Then correct each false statement to make it true.

_____ 1. Mass gatherings can present health problems because they decrease the spread of diseases.

   _____

_____ 2. The Saudi Arabian Ministry of Health has many years of experience managing people at the Olympic Games.

   _____

_____ 3. The yearly Hajj brings together about two million people every year.

   _____

_____ 4. The pilgrims are from Saudi Arabia.

   _____

_____ 5. During Hajj, when pilgrims arrive by plane, they must have a health screening.

   _____

_____ 6. In 2008, there was an outbreak of the H1N1 flu.

_____

_____ 7. New technology is very helpful in tracking and reporting doctors.

_____

_____ 8. The special field of health for mass gatherings depends on international cooperation.

_____

D. Complete the paragraphs below with details from the reading.

Large gatherings of people are dangerous because diseases can

spread _____ and _____ . But doctors
              1   2

from around the world are _____ their knowledge. Many
                             3

pilgrims to the Hajj have had little _____ care. So health
                             4

officials first provide a health _____ . There is a medical
                             5

_____ at the airport for pilgrims who are sick. The officials
         6

want to reduce the _____ of diseases spreading.
                      7

Saudi officials use _____ to track the outbreak of diseases.
                      8

They work with the World Health _____ to use rapid testing.
                             9

Health for mass gatherings is a new _____ of medicine.
                            10

E. What is the author's purpose in this reading? More than one answer is possible.
  a. to tell an interesting story
  b. to make the reader laugh
  c. to give information
  d. to explain a situation
  e. to make the reader excited about the topic

WRITE WHAT YOU THINK

A. Discuss these questions in a group. Look back at your Quick Write on page 181 as you think about what you learned.

1. Many people attend mass gatherings even if they are sick. Does this surprise you? Do you think that this should be permitted?

2. What else can doctors and other health care workers do at mass gatherings to help stop the spread of disease?

 ONLINE

B. Go online to watch the video about avian bird flu. Then check your comprehension.

CDC *(n.)* Centers for Disease Control and Prevention, a U.S. government organization

sustained *(adj.)* continuous

vulnerable *(adj.)* weak and easily hurt physically or emotionally

Critical Thinking **Tip**

Activity C asks you to **recommend** ways to prevent a problem. **Recommending** can help you think through a problem and its possible solutions.

C. Think about the unit video, Reading 1, and Reading 2 as you discuss these questions. Then choose one question and write a response.

1. Imagine that an epidemic spreads quickly and becomes a global pandemic. What kinds of problems do you think governments and doctors will face?

2. The flu can spread rapidly in schools and cause teachers and children to become sick. What can a school do to prevent the spread of the flu? When should a school close due to sickness?

Vocabulary Skill   Collocations

A **collocation** is a group of words that frequently go together. Some collocations are made up of a verb + a preposition. Here are some common collocations with the prepositions *on*, *to*, and *in*.

> comment on: to give an opinion about something
>
> contribute to: to give a part to the total of something
>
> in common: like or similar to somebody or something
>
> increase in: a rise in the number, amount, or level of something
>
> in favor of: in agreement with someone or something
>
> in response to: an answer or reaction to something
>
> participate in: to share or join in
>
> succeed in: to manage to achieve what you want; to do well

Using collocations will help your speaking and writing sound more natural.

A. Complete each sentence below with the correct collocation.

comment on	in common	in favor of	participate in
contribute to	increase in	in response to	succeed in

1. A cold and the flu have some things _____. For example, they can both be passed from one person to another.

2. My mother told me she liked my new dress, but she didn't _____ my new haircut. Maybe she doesn't like it.

3. The scientists need 50 people to _____ a study for a new flu vaccine. They will pay each person $500.

4. There's been a(n) _____ cases of the flu this winter. It's much worse than last year.

5. Eating lots of green vegetables can _____ your overall health.

6. Sofia nodded her head _____ my question.

7. If you want to _____ becoming an Olympic athlete, you have to train very hard.

8. Keiko was not _____ the new proposal, so she voted against it.

B. Choose five collocations from Activity A. Write a sentence using each one. Then share your sentences with a group.

 C. Go online for more practice with collocations.

WRITING

At the end of this unit, you will create an FAQ (Frequently Asked Questions) page that begins with an explanatory paragraph about an illness. This FAQ page will include specific information from the readings and your own ideas.

Writing Skill   Writing an explanatory paragraph

An **explanatory paragraph** defines and explains a term or concept. Use an explanatory paragraph when you want to explain a term or concept that your reader might not know.

Use these guidelines to make your explanatory paragraph clear to your reader.

- First, write a topic sentence that states and defines the term or concept.
- Make sure the definition is clear. Use a dictionary or online sources.
- Then write about the term or concept using explanations and examples.
- Explain how the term or concept is different from similar terms.
- Explain what the term or concept is not.

You can use these sentence structures to write a topic sentence for an explanatory paragraph.

_____ is a _____ that _____.

An <u>inhaler</u> is a <u>device</u> that <u>helps a person with asthma breathe</u>.

_____ is when _____.

An <u>epidemic</u> is when <u>many people have an illness at the same time</u>.

A. **WRITING MODEL** Read the model explanatory paragraph. Then answer the questions on page 188.

A pandemic is an epidemic that has spread to several countries or continents, becoming a global health emergency. An epidemic can develop into a pandemic very quickly. For example, in 2003, the SARS (Severe Acute Respiratory Syndrome) virus spread from China to 37 countries around the world in just a few weeks. The avian flu caused a pandemic in recent years. In 2009, a new type of flu virus started in Mexico and spread to 70 countries in eight weeks. A month later, the number of countries nearly doubled. A pandemic is not the same as a plague, which is a disease that spreads quickly and kills many people. A pandemic can kill many people, but it doesn't always. However, a pandemic is a very serious international health emergency.

1. What is the definition of *pandemic*?

   _____

2. What term is *pandemic* similar to?

   _____

3. What examples of pandemics does the writer give?

   _____

4. What does the writer say a pandemic is not?

   _____

5. Compare the paragraph on page 187 with paragraph 1 in Reading 1 on
   page 174. How are the paragraphs similar? How are they different?

   _____

B. Write a topic sentence for an explanatory paragraph for each of these
   topics. Use the two different sentence structures in the skill box on
   page 187. You may also need to look in the dictionary.

1. A common cold _____

   _____

2. An epidemic _____

   _____

3. Asthma _____

   _____

4. A vaccination _____

   _____

C. Complete each of the sentences related to the four topics in Activity B.
   The sentences will help explain your topic by saying what it is NOT or by
   using contrast.

1. _A common cold_ is not the same as the flu, _which is_ a more severe illness.

2. Although _____ is similar to the flu, flu

   symptoms are more _____.

3. Like _____, a pandemic is the spread of an infectious disease. However, in _____, the number of people affected is much smaller.

4. _____ is not the same as bronchitis, _____ a very bad cough. Unlike _____, bronchitis is treated with antibiotics.

5. A _____ is a special type of medicine, while *injection* refers to any type of medicine that is given with a needle under the skin. In fact, there are some _____ that are given by mouth, not by injection.

Writing **Tip**

In Activity D, you will complete an idea map to brainstorm ideas. Brainstorming ideas in this way will result in better writing.

D. Choose one of the topics in Activity B and complete the idea map to plan your writing. For examples, you can list symptoms or characteristics, depending on your topic.

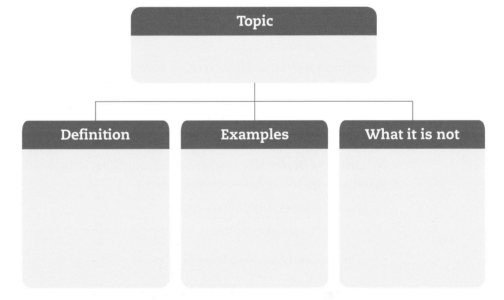

E. Write your explanatory paragraph. Use the guidelines in the Writing Skill box, topics from Activity B, and your idea map in Activity D.

F. Share your paragraph with another student who wrote about the same topic. Compare your paragraphs. Discuss these questions.

1. How are your topic sentences different? Which topic sentence is stronger? Why?

2. How many examples are in each of your paragraphs? Which examples are similar?

_____

3. Compare each other's sentences that say what your topic is not. How are they different? How do you think this information helps the reader?

_____

G. Work together with your partner to write a new explanatory paragraph. Use the best parts of each of your paragraphs.

 H. Go online for more practice with explanatory paragraphs.

Grammar | **Adverbs of manner and degree**

An **adverb of manner** describes how something is done or how something happens. It usually comes after the verb or object.

> Our team played **hard** and won the game **easily**.
>   verb   adverb   verb   object adverb

In sentences with an auxiliary verb, -*ly* adverbs of manner can come between the auxiliary verb and the main verb.

> His temperature was **rapidly** rising during the afternoon.
>   auxiliary   adverb verb

An **adverb of degree** tells to what degree something is done or happens. It comes before an adjective or before another adverb.

> It was an **especially** difficult exam.
>   adverb   adjective

> The man was breathing **fairly** slowly.
>   adverb adverb

Here are some common adverbs of degree:

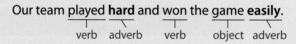

greater degree   **lesser degree**

extremely especially very really so fairly quite pretty somewhat hardly

A. Write the adverb form of each of the adjectives below. Then complete the sentences with the correct adverb of manner.

common _____	precise _____
efficient _____	rapid ____rapidly____
frequent _____	serious _____
immediate _____	successful _____

1. The temperature in New York can change very ____rapidly____. One day it's warm. The next day it's cold.

2. Doctors have not been able to _____ cure the common cold.

3. Modern cars use fuel more _____ than older cars do.

4. Hatem followed the instructions _____, because he didn't want to make a mistake.

5. Maria talks to her family _____. She calls them three or four times a week.

6. I need to think about the situation very _____ before I make a decision.

7. The doctor told Anita that her problem was serious. She needed to go to the hospital _____.

8. Orange trees are not _____ found in cold places.

Tip for Success

Don't overuse the adverbs *very* and *really*. They are useful general terms, but more specific adverbs give more information and make your writing more interesting.

B. Complete the sentences with your own ideas and opinions. Then read your sentences to a partner.

1. I think _____ is really interesting.

2. In my opinion _____ is extremely _____.

3. I can _____ fairly well.

4. For me _____ is extremely difficult.

5. I have had a(n) _____ _____ day today.

C. Go online for more practice with adverbs of manner and degree.

D. Go online for the grammar expansion.

In this assignment, you will write an FAQ (Frequently Asked Questions) page about an illness. You will include an explanation of the topic and information on how the illness can be prevented. As you prepare your FAQ page, think about the Unit Question, "How can we prevent diseases?" Use information from Reading 1, Reading 2, the unit video, and your work in this unit to support your writing. Refer to the Self-Assessment checklist on page 194.

Go to the Online Writing Tutor for a writing model and alternate Unit Assignments.

PLAN AND WRITE

A. **BRAINSTORM** **Complete these activities.**

1. Brainstorm a list for each question. Write down as many ideas as you can.
   - What illnesses do you know of that can spread from person to person?
   - What are some illnesses that you or someone you know have had?
   - What illnesses have you learned about recently?

2. Discuss your ideas with a partner.

3. Choose the illness you are going to write about.

Tip for Success

When you write an FAQ page, keep your audience in mind. Your questions should be questions that the average person might have. Your answers should be informative, but not too long. Be sure to include useful and interesting information that a reader may not know.

B. **PLAN** **Organize the information about your topic. Remember, your goal is to provide useful information to your readers.**

1. Fill in these FAQs with the illness you chose. Then write notes to answer each question.

   a. What is _____?

   _____

   _____

   b. What are the symptoms of _____?

   _____

   _____

   c. How is _____ different from other diseases?

   _____

   _____

d. Who gets _____?

_____

_____

e. How does _____ spread?

_____

_____

f. How can you avoid getting _____?

_____

_____

g. How can we prevent the spread of _____?

_____

_____

2. Look at your notes. Are there any questions you will not include? Are there any additional questions that you want to include? Make any changes needed.

3. What additional information do you need? Where can you get that information? Find the information you need and add it to your notes.

C. **WRITE** Use your **PLAN** notes to write your FAQ page. Go to *iQ Online* to use the Online Writing Tutor.

1. Write your FAQ page, using your notes in Activity B. Start with an explanatory paragraph that clearly explains the illness. Then continue with other questions and answers. Try to use some adverbs of manner and degree.

2. Look at the Self-Assessment checklist on page 194 to guide your writing.

REVISE AND EDIT

A. **PEER REVIEW** Read your partner's FAQ page. Then go online and use the Peer Review worksheet. Discuss the review with your partner.

B. **REWRITE** Based on your partner's review, revise and rewrite your paragraph.

C. **EDIT** Complete the Self-Assessment checklist as you prepare to write the final draft of your FAQ page. Be prepared to hand in your work or discuss it in class.

SELF-ASSESSMENT		
Yes	**No**	
☐	☐	Did you clearly define the illness with explanations and examples?
☐	☐	Do you have a good variety of adverbs of manner and degree? Did you use the correct word order?
☐	☐	Did you use collocations to make your writing sound more natural?
☐	☐	Does the FAQ page include vocabulary from the unit?
☐	☐	Did you check the FAQ page for punctuation, spelling, and grammar?

D. **REFLECT** Go to the Online Discussion Board to discuss these questions.

1. What is something new you learned in this unit?

2. Look back at the Unit Question—How can we prevent diseases? Is your answer different now than when you started the unit? If yes, how is it different? Why?

TRACK YOUR SUCCESS

Circle the words and phrases you have learned in this unit.

Nouns
cooperation 🔑 AWL
decade 🔑 AWL
epidemic
outbreak
risk 🔑
strategy 🔑 AWL
symptom
vaccination
virus 🔑

Verbs
cover 🔑
develop 🔑

infect 🔑
quarantine
track 🔑

Adjectives
mass 🔑
severe 🔑

Adverbs
approximately 🔑 AWL
extremely 🔑

Phrasal Verbs
take steps

Collocations
comment on
contribute to
in common
increase in
in favor of
in response to
participate in
related to 🔑
succeed in

🔑 Oxford 3000™ words

AWL Academic Word List

Check (✓) the skills you learned. If you need more work on a skill, refer to the page(s) in parentheses.

READING ■	I can synthesize information. (p. 178)
VOCABULARY ■	I can use collocations. (p. 185)
WRITING ■	I can write an explanatory paragraph. (p. 187)
GRAMMAR ■	I can use adverbs of manner and degree. (p. 190)
UNIT OBJECTIVE ▶▶▶▶	■ I can gather information and ideas to create an FAQ page that begins with an explanatory paragraph about an illness.

AUTHORS AND CONSULTANTS

Authors

Joe McVeigh holds a B.A. in English and American Literature from Brown University and an M.A. in TESOL from Biola University. He has taught at Middlebury College, the University of Southern California, the California Institute of Technology, and California State University, Los Angeles. Joe has also lived and worked overseas in the U.K., Hungary, China, India, Chile, and the Middle East. He has presented nationally and internationally on topics including methods and techniques for teaching English, intercultural communication, and curriculum development. He works independently as a consultant, teacher-trainer, workshop presenter, and author.

Jennifer Bixby holds an M.A. in TESOL from Boston University. She is a senior development editor for EF Englishtown, editing and writing online ELT content. Jennifer has taught students of various ages in Colombia, Japan, and the U.S in a wide variety of programs, including community colleges and intensive English programs. She has presented at numerous conferences on the topics of materials development and the teaching of reading and writing. She is coauthor with Nigel Caplan of *Inside Writing* 2 and 4 published by Oxford University Press.

Series Consultants

ONLINE INTEGRATION

Chantal Hemmi holds an Ed.D. TEFL and is a Japan-based teacher trainer and curriculum designer. Since leaving her position as Academic Director of the British Council in Tokyo, she has been teaching at the Center for Language Education and Research at Sophia University on an EAP/CLIL program offered for undergraduates. She delivers lectures and teacher trainings throughout Japan, Indonesia, and Malaysia.

COMMUNICATIVE GRAMMAR

Nancy Schoenfeld holds an M.A. in TESOL from Biola University in La Mirada, California, and has been an English language instructor since 2000. She has taught ESL in California and Hawaii, and EFL in Thailand and Kuwait. She has also trained teachers in the United States and Indonesia. Her interests include teaching vocabulary, extensive reading, and student motivation. She is currently an English Language Instructor at Kuwait University.

WRITING

Marguerite Ann Snow holds a Ph.D. in Applied Linguistics from UCLA. She teaches in the TESOL M.A. program in the Charter College of Education at California State University, Los Angeles. She was a Fulbright scholar in Hong Kong and Cyprus. In 2006, she received the President's Distinguished Professor award at Cal State, LA. She has trained EFL teachers in Algeria, Argentina, Brazil, Egypt, Libya, Morocco, Pakistan, Peru, Spain, and Turkey. She is the author/editor of publications in the areas of integrated content, English for academic purposes, and standards for English teaching and learning. She recently served as a co-editor of *Teaching English as a Second or Foreign Language* (4th ed.).

VOCABULARY

Cheryl Boyd Zimmerman is a Professor at California State University, Fullerton. She specializes in second-language vocabulary acquisition, an area in which she is widely published. She teaches graduate courses on second-language acquisition, culture, vocabulary, and the fundamentals of TESOL and is a frequent invited speaker on topics related to vocabulary teaching and learning. She is the author of *Word Knowledge: A Vocabulary Teacher's Handbook* and Series Director of *Inside Reading, Inside Writing*, and *Inside Listening and Speaking,* all published by Oxford University Press.

ASSESSMENT

Lawrence J. Zwier holds an M.A. in TESL from the University of Minnesota. He is currently the Associate Director for Curriculum Development at the English Language Center at Michigan State University in East Lansing. He has taught ESL/EFL in the United States, Saudi Arabia, Malaysia, Japan, and Singapore.

iQ ONLINE extends your learning beyond the classroom. This online content is specifically designed for you! *iQ Online* gives you flexible access to essential content.

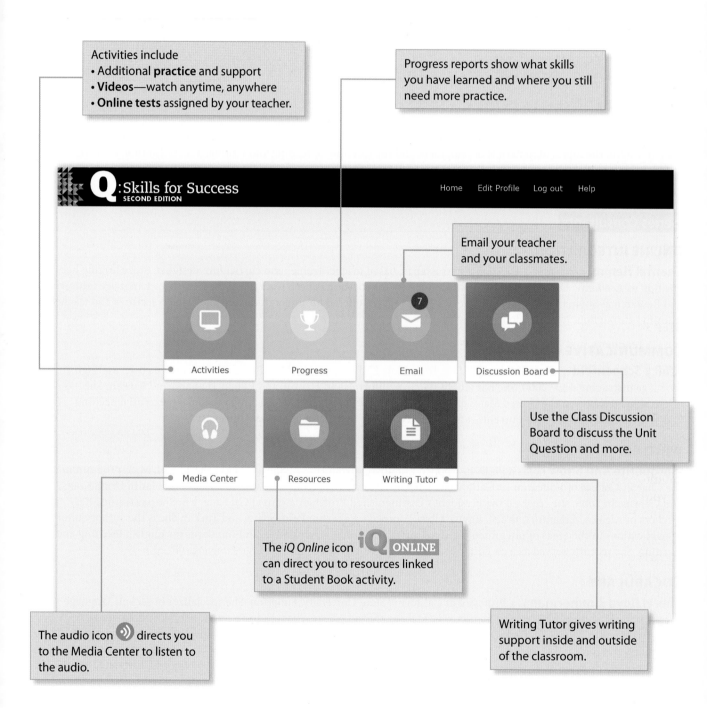

Activities include
• Additional **practice** and support
• **Videos**—watch anytime, anywhere
• **Online tests** assigned by your teacher.

Progress reports show what skills you have learned and where you still need more practice.

Email your teacher and your classmates.

Use the Class Discussion Board to discuss the Unit Question and more.

The *iQ Online* icon **iQ ONLINE** can direct you to resources linked to a Student Book activity.

The audio icon directs you to the Media Center to listen to the audio.

Writing Tutor gives writing support inside and outside of the classroom.

SEE THE INSIDE FRONT COVER FOR HOW TO REGISTER FOR *iQ ONLINE* FOR THE FIRST TIME.

Take Control of Your Learning

You have the choice of where and how you complete the activities. Access your activities and view your progress at any time.

Your teacher may

- assign *iQ Online* as homework,
- do the activities with you in class, or
- let you complete the activities at a pace that is right for you.

iQ Online makes it easy to access everything you need.

Set Clear Goals

STEP 1 If it is your first time, look through the site. See what learning opportunities are available.

STEP 2 The Student Book provides the framework and purpose for each online activity. Before going online, notice the goal of the exercises you are going to do.

STEP 3 Stay on top of your work, following the teacher's instructions.

STEP 4 Use *iQ Online* for review. You can use the materials any time. It is easy for you to do follow-up activities when you have missed a class or want to review.

Manage Your Progress

The activities in *iQ Online* are designed for you to work independently. You can become a confident learner by monitoring your progress and reviewing the activities at your own pace. You may already be used to working online, but if you are not, go to your teacher for guidance.

Check 'View Reports' to monitor your progress. The reports let you track your own progress at a glance. Think about your own performance and set new goals that are right for you, following the teacher's instructions.

iQ Online is a research-based solution specifically designed for English language learners that extends learning beyond the classroom. I hope these steps help you make the most of this essential content.

C. N. Hemmi

Chantal Hemmi, EdD TEFL
Center for Language Education and Research
Sophia University, Japan

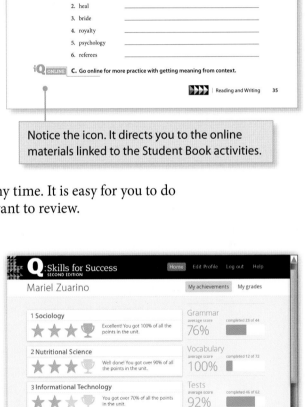

Reading Skill Getting meaning from context

If you find a word you don't know in a text, you can use the **context** to help you understand the meaning of the word. The context is the other words near the unknown word.

It was a **joyful** celebration. Everyone was very happy.

The red sign told me that there was **danger** and some possibility of injury.

From the context, you can understand that the word *joyful* means "very happy." From the example, you can understand that *danger* means "a chance that someone might get hurt."

Critical Thinking Tip
In Activities A and B, you will use the context to understand the meaning of new words. Using context to guess meaning can help you read more fluently.

A. Read these sentences from Reading 1. Circle the words that give the context for the bold word in each sentence.

1. Those colors may give us a **feeling** of warmth and comfort or feelings of anger.
2. Ancient cultures in China, Egypt, and India used colors to **heal** sicknesses. For example, people used blue to decrease pain.
3. In the United States, white represents goodness. It is usually the color of a **bride**'s wedding dress.
4. In European cultures, purple is the color of **royalty** for kings and queens.
5. Color **psychology** is the study of how colors affect our emotions.
6. Soccer **referees** made more decisions against teams that wore black uniforms.

B. Write a definition for each word from Activity A. Then check your definitions in your dictionary.

1. feeling _____
2. heal _____
3. bride _____
4. royalty _____
5. psychology _____
6. referees _____

C. Go online for more practice with getting meaning from context.

Reading and Writing   35

Notice the icon. It directs you to the online materials linked to the Student Book activities.

Q: *Skills for Success Second Edition* audio can be found in the Media Center.

Follow these steps:

Step 1: Go to iQOnlinePractice.com.

Step 2: Click on the Media Center icon. 🎧

Step 3: Choose to stream or download ⬇ the audio file you select. Not all audio files are available for download.

Class Audio

Unit	Page	Listen	Download
Unit 1			
1	3	The Q Classroom	⬇
1	6	Work With the Reading	⬇
1	13	Work With the Reading	⬇
Unit 2			
2	28	The Q Classroom	⬇
2	32	Work With the Reading	⬇
2	38	Work With the Reading	⬇
Unit 3			
3	55	The Q Classroom	⬇
3	58	Work With the Reading	⬇
3	65	Work With the Reading	

Back

Unit	Activity	Track File Name
Unit 1	The Q Classroom, p. 3	Q2e_02_RW_U01_Q_Classroom.mp3
	Work With the Reading, p. 6	Q2e_02_RW_U01_ Reading1.mp3
	Work With the Reading, p. 12	Q2e_02_RW_U01_Reading2.mp3
Unit 2	The Q Classroom, p. 26	Q2e_02_RW_U02_Q_Classroom.mp3
	Work With the Reading, p. 31	Q2e_02_RW_U02_Reading1.mp3
	Work With the Reading, p. 37	Q2e_02_RW_U02_Reading2.mp3
Unit 3	The Q Classroom, p. 50	Q2e_02_RW_U03_Q_Classroom.mp3
	Work With the Reading, p. 54	Q2e_02_RW_U03_Reading1.mp3
	Work With the Reading, p. 61	Q2e_02_RW_U03_Reading2.mp3
Unit 4	The Q Classroom, p. 74	Q2e_02_RW_U04_Q_Classroom.mp3
	Work With the Reading, p. 78	Q2e_02_RW_U04_Reading1.mp3
	Work With the Reading, p. 85	Q2e_02_RW_U04_Reading2.mp3
Unit 5	The Q Classroom, p. 99	Q2e_02_RW_U05_Q_Classroom.mp3
	Work With the Reading, p. 103	Q2e_02_RW_U05_Reading1.mp3
	Work With the Reading, p. 109	Q2e_02_RW_U05_Reading2.mp3
Unit 6	The Q Classroom, p. 123	Q2e_02_RW_U06_Q_Classroom.mp3
	Work With the Reading, p. 126	Q2e_02_RW_U06_Reading1.mp3
	Work With the Reading, p. 133	Q2e_02_RW_U06_Reading2.mp3
Unit 7	The Q Classroom, p. 146	Q2e_02_RW_U07_Q_Classroom.mp3
	Work With the Reading, p. 151	Q2e_02_RW_U07_Reading1.mp3
	Work With the Reading, p. 158	Q2e_02_RW_U07_Reading2.mp3
Unit 8	The Q Classroom, p. 171	Q2e_02_RW_U08_Q_Classroom.mp3
	Work With the Reading, p. 174	Q2e_02_RW_U08_Reading1.mp3
	Work With the Reading, p. 182	Q2e_02_RW_U08_Reading2.mp3

🔑 The keywords of the **Oxford 3000**™ have been carefully selected by a group of language experts and experienced teachers as the words which should receive priority in vocabulary study because of their importance and usefulness.

AWL **The Academic Word List** is the most principled and widely accepted list of academic words. Averil Coxhead gathered information from academic materials across the academic disciplines to create this word list.

The Common European Framework of Reference for Languages (CEFR) provides a basic description of what language learners have to do to use language effectively. The system contains 6 reference levels: **A1, A2, B1, B2, C1, C2.** CEFR leveling provided by the Word Family Framework, created by Richard West and published by the British Council. http://www.learnenglish.org.uk/wff/

UNIT 1

clear *(adj.)* 🔑, A1
connect *(v.)* 🔑, A2
contribute *(v.)* 🔑 AWL, A2
express *(v.)* 🔑, A1
find out *(phr. v.)*, A2
influence *(v.)* 🔑, A2
psychologist *(n.)* AWL, B1
purchase *(n.)* 🔑 AWL, B1
recommend *(v.)* 🔑, A2
researcher *(n.)* AWL, A2
review *(n.)* 🔑, A2
social *(adj.)* 🔑, A1
spread *(v.)* 🔑, A2
study *(n.)* 🔑, A1
trend *(n.)* 🔑 AWL, A2

UNIT 2

advertising *(n.)* 🔑, B1
affect *(v.)* 🔑 AWL, A1
consider *(v.)* 🔑, A1
culture *(n.)* 🔑 AWL, A1
dependable *(adj.)*, B1
emotion *(n.)* 🔑, A2
encourage *(v.)* 🔑, A1
environment *(n.)* 🔑 AWL, A1
establish *(v.)* 🔑 AWL, A1
psychological *(adj.)* AWL, B1

represent *(v.)* 🔑, B1
service *(n.)* 🔑, A2
specific *(adj.)* 🔑 AWL, A1
unaware *(adj.)* AWL, B2
universal *(adj.)* 🔑, B1
variety *(n.)* 🔑, A1

UNIT 3

advice *(n.)* 🔑, A2
avoid *(v.)* 🔑, A1
awkward *(adj.)* 🔑, B2
manners *(n.)*, B2
appropriately *(adv.)* AWL, B2
behavior *(n.)* 🔑, A1
custom *(n.)* 🔑, A2
firmly *(adv.)* 🔑, B1
informal *(adj.)* 🔑, B1
interrupt *(v.)* 🔑, B1
make a good impression
     (phr. v.), B2
gesture *(n.)*, B1
respect *(n.)* 🔑, A2
take part in *(phr. v.)*, B1
traditional *(adj.)* 🔑 AWL, A1
typical *(adj.)* 🔑, A2

UNIT 4

advantage *(n.)* 🔑, A1
artificial *(adj.)* 🔑, B2

ban *(v.)* 🔑, B1
championship *(n.)*, A2
compete *(v.)* 🔑, A2
effect *(n.)* 🔑, A1
energy *(n.)* 🔑 AWL, A2
equipment *(n.)* 🔑 AWL, A1
financial *(adj.)* 🔑 AWL, A1
include *(v.)* 🔑, A1
invent *(v.)* 🔑, B1
limit *(n.)* 🔑, A2
performance *(n.)* 🔑, B1
reason *(n.)* 🔑, A1
solution *(n.)* 🔑, A2
technology *(n.)* 🔑 AWL, A1

UNIT 5

challenge *(n.)* 🔑 AWL, A2
corporation *(n.)* AWL, B1
courage *(n.)* 🔑, B2
depend on *(phr. v.)* 🔑, A2
design *(v.)* 🔑 AWL, A1
enthusiasm *(n.)* 🔑, B1
expand *(v.)* 🔑 AWL, A2
expert *(n.)* 🔑 AWL, A2
goal *(n.)* 🔑 AWL, A2
lifestyle *(n.)*, B2
manage *(v.)* 🔑, A1
pass down *(phr. v.)*, B1

realistic *(adj.)* 🔑, B1
responsibility *(n.)* 🔑, A1
strength *(n.)* 🔑, A1
talent *(n.)* 🔑, B1
unity *(n.)*, B1

UNIT 6

automatically *(adv.)* 🔑 AWL, B1
access *(n.)* 🔑 AWL, A1
assist *(v.)* 🔑 AWL, B1
benefit *(n.)* 🔑 AWL, A1
blame *(v.)* 🔑, A2
connection *(n.)* 🔑, B1
decrease *(v.)* 🔑, B1
error *(n.)* 🔑 AWL, A2
estimate *(v.)* 🔑 AWL, A2
eventually *(adv.)* 🔑 AWL, A1
frustrated *(adj.)*, B2
furious *(adj.)*, B2
install *(v.)* 🔑, B1
interact *(v.)* AWL, B2
on hold *(phr.)*, B2
provide *(v.)* 🔑, A1
scan *(v.)*, B2

stressed *(adj.)* 🔑 AWL, B1
transfer *(v.)* 🔑 AWL, B1
unique *(adj.)* 🔑 AWL, A2

UNIT 7

actual *(adj.)* 🔑, A2
attitude *(n.)* 🔑 AWL, A1
budget *(n.)* 🔑, A1
consequences *(n.)* 🔑 AWL, A2
consumer *(n.)* 🔑 AWL, A1
disposable *(adj.)* AWL, B1
exist *(v.)* 🔑, A1
factor *(n.)* 🔑 AWL, A1
feature *(n.)* 🔑 AWL, A1
fresh *(adj.)* 🔑, A2
habit *(n.)* 🔑, B1
materialistic *(adj.)*, B2
model *(n.)* 🔑, A2
patched *(adj.)*, B2
persuade *(v.)* 🔑, A2
possession *(n.)* 🔑, B2
sign *(n.)* 🔑, A2
significant *(adj.)* 🔑 AWL, A1
term *(n.)* 🔑, A2

UNIT 8

approximately *(adv.)* 🔑 AWL, B1
cooperation *(n.)* 🔑 AWL, B1
cover *(v.)* 🔑, A2
decade *(n.)* 🔑 AWL, A2
develop *(v.)* 🔑, A1
epidemic *(n.)*, C1
extremely *(adv.)* 🔑, A2
infect *(v.)* 🔑, B1
mass *(adj.)* 🔑, B1
outbreak *(n.)*, C1
quarantine *(v.)*, C1
related to *(adj.)* 🔑, B1
risk *(n.)* 🔑, A1
strategy *(n.)* 🔑 AWL, A1
severe *(adj.)* 🔑, A2
symptom *(n.)*, B1
take steps *(phr. v.)*, A2
track *(v.)* 🔑, B1
vaccination *(n.)*, C1
virus *(n.)* 🔑, B1

OXFORD
UNIVERSITY PRESS

198 Madison Avenue
New York, NY 10016 USA

Great Clarendon Street, Oxford, OX2 6DP, United Kingdom

Oxford University Press is a department of the University of Oxford.
It furthers the University's objective of excellence in research, scholarship,
and education by publishing worldwide. Oxford is a registered trade
mark of Oxford University Press in the UK and in certain other countries

Director, ELT New York: Laura Pearson
Head of Adult, ELT New York: Stephanie Karras
Publisher: Sharon Sargent
Managing Editor: Mariel DeKranis
Development Editor: Eric Zuarino
Executive Art and Design Manager: Maj-Britt Hagsted
Design Project Manager: Debbie Lofaso
Content Production Manager: Julie Armstrong
Senior Production Artist: Elissa Santos
Image Manager: Trisha Masterson
Image Editor: Liaht Ziskind
Production Coordinator: Brad Tucker

ISBN: 978 0 19 481876 6 Student Book 2B with iQ Online pack
ISBN: 978 0 19 481877 3 Student Book 2B as pack component
ISBN: 978 0 19 481802 5 iQ Online student website

Printed in China
This book is printed on paper from certified and well-managed sources.

ACKNOWLEDGEMENTS

*The authors and publisher are grateful to those who have given permission to
reproduce the following extracts and adaptations of copyright material:*

p. 31 "The Color of Business" from "What Color Is Business?" by Orwig
Marketing Strategies. Copyright © 2004 Orwig Marketing Strategies,
http://www.orwig.net/articles/what_color/what_color.html. Used by
permission; p. 133 "I Hate Machines!" from "Self-Service World" by
Sheila Moss, http://www.humorcolumnist.com. Copyright Sheila Moss.
Used by permission; p. 158 from "In Praise of the Throwaway Society"
by Anthony Forte, http://www.madanthony.net. Used by permission of
the author.

Illustrations by: p. 76 Stuart Bradford; p. 86 5W Infographics; p. 126 Claudia
Carlson; p. 148 Karen Minot; Inside Back Cover: Ivcandy/Getty Images/
Bloom Design/ Shutterstock.

*We would also like to thank the following for permission to reproduce the following
photographs:* Cover: Yongyut Kumsri/Shutterstock; Video Vocabulary (used
throughout the book): Oleksiy Mark / Shutterstock; p. 2 Ian Dagnall/
Alamy; p. 2/3 ericlefrancais/Shutterstock; p. 3 DrAfter123/iStockphoto
(media); p. 3 gbrundin/iStockphoto (listening); p. 6 Red Bull Content Pool/
Rex Features; p. 7 Courtesy of Tom Dickson and Blendtec/Blendtec; p.
12 RichardBakerNews/Alamy; p. 13 Bloomberg/Getty Images; p. 26/27
Yongyut Kumsri/Shutterstock; p. 28 Tina Tyrell/Corbis Outline/Corbis UK
Ltd. (blue); p. 28 Tina Tyrell/Corbis Outline/Corbis UK Ltd. (brown); p. 28
Tina Tyrell/Corbis Outline/Corbis UK Ltd. (green); p. 28 Adam Blasberg/
Getty Images (red); p. 32 Henry Westheim Photography/Alamy; p. 37 Jim
West/Alamy; p. 41 Chris Rout/Alamy; p. 50/51 Brand New Images/Getty
Images; p. 54 Age Fotostock /Superstock Ltd.; p. 55 danishkhan /iStockphoto
(greeting); p. 55 Milk Photographie/Corbis UK Ltd. (gift); p. 61 David R.
Frazier Photolibrary, Inc./Alamy; p. 74/75 Stefan Holm/Shutterstock; p. 79
Natursports/Shutterstock; p. 85 Caiaimage/Rex Features; p. 98 mearicon/
Shutterstock (tools); p. 98 ColorBlind Images Blend Images/Newscom (father
son); p. 99 Jim Goldstein Danita Delimont Photography/Newscom (sign); p.
99 Hurst Photo/Shutterstock (calculator); p. 100 amana images inc./Alamy
(family); p. 100 stockstudioX/Getty Images (kitchen); p. 100 Celia Peterson/
Getty Images (mother daughters); p. 100 Ken Seet/Corbis UK Ltd. (tucking
in); p. 103 Radius Images/Alamy; p. 104 2013 The Washington Post/Getty
Images; p. 109 Kristoffer Tripplaar/Alamy (sale); p. 109 Jerry Arcieri/Corbis
UK Ltd. (wall street); p. 122 Kevin Foy/Alamy; p. 123 master2/iStockphoto
(atm); p. 123 Alexandru Nika/Shutterstock (code); p. 124 Tim Boyle/Getty
Images (self-service); p. 124 Alex Segre/Alamy (tesco); p. 124 Henry George
Beeker/Alamy (airport); p. 124 Richard Levine/Alamy (gas); p. 134 Andres
Rodriguez/Alamy; p. 138 corepics/Fotolia; p. 139 Hugh Sitton/Corbis UK Ltd.;
p. 146/147 Jon Hicks/Corbis UK Ltd.; p. 151 Caro /Alamy (repair); p. 151 Peter
Crome/Alamy (mobile phones); p. 152 Photodisc/Oxford University Press;
p. 170 Matej Kastelic/Shutterstock; p. 170/171 piotr_pabijan/Shutterstock;
p. 171 OpenFlights (map); p. 171 Zoom Team/Shutterstock (fruit); p. 172
Halfdark/Getty Images (ill); p. 172 Nigel Cattlin /Alamy (mosquito); p. 172
Jose Luis Pelaez/Blend Images//Corbis UK Ltd. (xray); p. 172 Mark Hatfield/
Getty Images (test); p. 172 Brandon Tabiolo/Getty Images (sunscreen); p. 172
perfectmatch/Fotolia (inhaler).